MORE SPIT THAN POLISH

AT · TOLMAN · POND

MORE SPIT THAN POLISH

AT · TOLMAN · POND

An unlikely summer resort in the wilds of Nelson, New Hampshire, another "little town that Time forgot"

by F. B. Tolman

YANKEE BOOKS

A division of Yankee Publishing Incorporated
Dublin, New Hampshire

Edited by Clarissa Silitch
Designed by Jill Shaffer
Frontispiece by Roy Lewando

Yankee Publishing Incorporated
Dublin, New Hampshire 03444

First Edition

Library of Congress Cataloging-in-Publication Data

Tolman, F. B., 1902-
    More spit than polish at Tolman Pond.

    1. Nelson (N.H.) — Social life and customs.
2. Tolman, F. B., 1902-   3. Nelson (N.H.) —
Biography.   I. Title.
F44.N4T65   1987   974.2'9   87-6082
ISBN 0-89909-138-5

For Kirsten, Stacia, Ebenezer, and
Thomas — my grandchildren, Ma's great grandchildren,
and great-great-great-great grandchildren of the
first Ebenezer Tolman.

❧ Author's Note

THIS BOOK is not always strictly factual, but in essence it is all true, being a composite of tales I picked up hanging around Ma's kitchen waiting for a bowl of hot fish chowder (perch and hornpout caught in Tolman Pond, of course), listening to what was going on in Nelson and hearing what had gone on in the past, observing the passing characters who came in from the outside to add their color to the scene. Whatever has been recounted here has been done with affection, in gratitude to the Tolmans and to the people of Nelson.

CONTENTS

CHAPTER ONE

◆ *Good Running Water*

THE FARM at Tolman Pond was in a sorry state when Sadie and Wayland Tolman were married at the turn of the century. The farmhouse was already a hundred years old and looked every day of it. After they had lived there for fifty years, it looked much the same. The walls had popped a few more clapboards, the roof had a few more old-age wrinkles, and the porch had sagged lower under its tangled load of vines. Through the decades, sporadic attempts were made to shore up the foundations; in fact they are still holding up, and the house is still standing — leaning, perhaps, but up. The stubborn, slovenly, good-humored character of the place has endured.

None of this bothered Sadie when she married and never did later. What really mattered was that she now had what she had always wanted — a farm.

She had looked this one over the previous year when she was teaching in the Nelson School. If the farm was scrawny, so was the town, and she accepted it "as is" and with it Wayland. Spit and polish were not important. Sadie knew she could make the farm run, and she did. In its fashion.

Wayland had just one ambition when he married; he wanted Sadie to have the moon if that was what she hankered for. Because the particular moon she wanted happened to be the slatternly old farm left him by his father, he was in luck as that was all he had. In his eagerness he didn't feel called upon to point out that this moon was not made of the best cheese.

He was no farmer. A "rough" carpenter, he could slap together a henhouse with no trouble at all, never mind if there were feathers poking through the cracks. By providing Sadie with a farm, Wayland felt he had done his bit; from there on it was up to her. But there was to be no rocking chair for him. Ma regarded him as part of the creaking machinery on the place that had to be kept going somehow or other. She kept him moving, if slowly.

No matter how tenacious, how resolute a farmer Ma was (to Wayland she was always his "Sadie," to everyone else she became "Ma"), she was balked by land that had so little good soil, so many rocks, sour pastures and dilapidated barns. As a farm that could support itself, it was hopeless. Others in Nelson faced with the same conditions gave up and moved West. But Ma never considered giving up. The place had one asset — the pond in front. It was fed by two brooks, and good running water was rare. With that as a bonus there had to be some way to make the farm work. And Ma found it.

Instead of sheep and cattle, she stocked the place with boarders — good quality, even tempered, mold-resistant boarders. And the strain she introduced fifty years ago has proved to be of lasting value.

To ensure a consistently high standard, she tended her charges meticulously, careful not to weaken their physical or moral fiber by overindulgence. Her interest in their welfare was distinctly proprietary. She took over their lives. She assumed sovereignty.

For the summer months, Tolman Pond became the world to all those in Ma's fold. Her orbit encompassed them; she loomed large, a monumental figure in an apron. On their return in the fall to their winter quarters, it seemed incredible that no one had ever heard of Ma, of Tolman Pond, of Nelson, or even of New Hampshire.

It came as no surprise to a one-time boarder when touring in England to find a statue of Ma in London — Ma sitting hunched over, brooding. A plaque at the base of the statue claimed the figure to be Queen Victoria, but of course it was Ma — Ma in her sitting room brooding over her kitchen resources — Ma considering how to make those skimpy parsnips do for eleven boarders. It made the traveler homesick. As he looked, he heard a local voice nearby remark, "I seen 'er once. She were like a bit of brown pudding. But not a soft brown pudding — not softlike — no, she wa'ant soft . . . "

Neither was Ma. She wasn't even brown. But like the Queen, she had presence; she, too, was a benevolent monarch. They both were lucky in having amiable consorts — admiring, loving husbands. Neither man suffered or felt himself handicapped by having a dominant wife; each was content to sit back and let his lady steamroller out the bumps and lumps of sovereignty. Staunch, affectionate, comfortable, they stood to one side and held their tongues, giving silent, loyal support. The Queen had a vast staff — aides, ministers, flunkies. Ma too had a vast staff — all Mabel.

As Ma's initial plan had been to farm, she needed boys who would do the chores and develop into farmhands. Knowing there was only one way to get things done right, Ma produced her own, designed to her particular specifications, with, of course, the amiable cooperation of her husband. Here, she had a setback.

As youngsters, the two boys did chores agreeably enough, but their hearts weren't in it. After all, they weren't descended from Ma alone — Wayland had come into the act. Far from developing into stalwart farmhands who would willingly sweat in the fields from dawn to dark, they cared nothing for tilling the soil or for manhandling boulders out of the sour pastures. No indeed, they were all for leaving everything just as it was. They treated the cows they milked in an offhand, disrespectful manner, and whenever they were sent to gather eggs, they left the hens ruffled and furious, swearing never, never to lay another damned egg.

It was only later, when Ma switched from farming to boarders, that she got her money's worth from the boys. In the long run they proved to be a cash asset.

❦ Horsepower

IF THE farmhouse was not in top condition, neither was the town. The roads had originally been made by horses and oxen picking their way over the rough and bony land, working around boulders, finding the easy spot to cross a brook, accommodating the paths to the terrain. Speed was not important. Getting a load from one place to another without either laming or exhausting a team was. At that pace, farms and mills and the town itself had flourished.

However, as soon as the industrial age coughed and sputtered onto the scene, calling for straight roads and speedier travel, Nelson bogged down. It just didn't take to straightness or right angles or the shortest path between two points; none of that suited. The final blow was when the straight-running railroad came to the county seat of Keene, only a few miles away. That took the wind right out of the town. The few young men back from the war with the South looked over their wilting village, and one by one left on the train for greener pastures, or better yet, city streets with no pastures at all.

Nelson never shriveled up entirely, though it had a narrow escape. When Ma and Wayland were married, the population had shrunk from a high of several thousand to a mere four hundred. The town was reduced to a handful of cross-grained natives who couldn't be blasted loose. They hung on stubbornly, adding bits of barbed wire to their rusty fences, patching, grumbling and glaring at the "summer people" who were discovering Nelson in increasing numbers.

Charmed by the brushy quiet, the ponds and the timid, twisting brooks, the newcomers bought up and repaired the old farmhouses before they became heaps of rubble. It was the summer folk who unwittingly saved the town from extinction, but got no thanks for it.

At some period, it dawned on the natives still remaining that summer people were a crop from which they might harvest enough fodder to tide them through the lean winters. Rickety signs appeared on rickety houses — "Fresh Eggs," "Squashes for Sale" or "Guests." Summer people, boarders and natives learned to get along in a working relationship at least. Communication stopped there, for otherwise they just didn't speak the same language.

Fran Tolman and his brother Newt, though, were bilingual. Having attended the local school, they spoke the local jargon (not a dialect exactly, but it did have its own rhythm and timing). However, brought up in a household of Ma's boarders, they also picked up the accents and vocabulary heard there. They switched tongues according to where they were or whom they were with.

When my family came here as summer people (we rented a house about five miles from Tolman Pond), a number of Nelson's roads had been improved to accommodate cars. Not much improved, but some. The other old roads were almost invisible, out of sight to automobile drivers. But to people with saddle horses, that network of skeleton tracks was an invitation to trace the not-so-distant past.

Fran was Ma's eldest son, home for the summer from a year at a Boston art school. He had a horse, and I had a horse; we met at the blacksmith shop, and our horses proved congenial. It was Fran who introduced me to the maze of abandoned back roads between our homes. On horseback, we explored the web of grassed-over wooded trails that separated his world of deer tracks, ruins and fox runs from mine of suburban sidewalks and commuter trains. Thanks to those roads, those horses, I got a glimpse of an offbeat, backhanded country boarding house, the weedy empire ruled over by Sadie and her entourage (Mabel), and eventually became Ma's daughter-in-law, to the astonishment of us both.

Riding, Fran talked, and as we ambled along, I saw the town from horseback. In a car, I would have shot right by, and on foot (Fran hated to walk unless there was a purpose to it, such as shooting), I wouldn't have seen as much. Although my rented horse was of uncertain disposition, he behaved with perfect decorum while Fran unraveled for me the knotty fortunes of Nelson.

"See that cellar hole with the old apple trees around it? That's where the Osgoods used to live; at one time they had about a hundred sheep. It was a good-sized farm. All this," — Fran swept away the woods with his arm — "all this was open land, all fields. They said that the old grandfather got so he couldn't stand the cold any longer, and nights he'd hunker down with the sheep. He spent so much time with those sheep he had wool in his beard, coming out of his nose, sticking out of the tops of his boots. When he went to the store, to do his trading, he had first to work his mouth out of its woolly insulation before he could get his words going, and then he'd sound like this . . ." and here Fran's voice fell to a staccato stutter, " 'A-a need baa-naan-a-as and baa-a-con, and a ba-a-g of — ,' but by that time the storekeeper was already setting out his usual order — bacon, bananas, lamp wicks, cornmeal, snuff and the half-gallon of rum the old man had to have to keep the juice running in his thin, old veins."

Fran pulled his horse's head out of the bushes he was munching on and started along, but I stopped.

"How long ago was that? How long ago was there still a house here?"

"There was still some of the house here when I was a kid, probably well over a hundred years old by then. That old guy I was telling you about was a brother-in-law of my grandfather's. They both joined up at the same time and went to the Civil War together. They didn't see much fighting because they both got sick of fever and had a bad time. When they finally came home, they were in poor shape, and never really got over it. Their farms were run down, and they didn't have the strength to start over. Just lost heart, I guess."

"And now there's nothing left, nothing at all. I should think there'd be some timbers or boards or something . . . "

"Once the roof goes, everything rots away fast. And then people took away anything useful — wood, bricks, whatever. Even pried up the stone lintels and doorsteps. Only the cellar hole is left. It's hard to steal a cellar hole."

"So the whole family just disappeared without a trace, nothing?"

"Well, the apple trees are here and the lilacs. All that myrtle there was where the front doorstep was; that's still here and spreading. They kept it nice, once, you know. It was pretty."

A few years later I went back and dug up some patches of myrtle and some lilacs. Now I have Osgood roots by my

doorstep. In the early spring, the bushes sprout tufts of woolly white.

Other days on the trails were patterned with anecdotes
like:

"Saw a partridge with six chicks right here last year."

"See that signpost? When I was seven, I got a new jackknife for my birthday. When I tried to knock an apple off that
post with it, I missed. I looked and looked, then I'd come back
and look again, but I never did find that jackknife. Here, just
hold my horse, I'll poke around in those bushes. It's got to be
*some*where."

"Right here, right near this oak, is where old Frank's
great-uncle saw some bear tracks and followed them. When
he didn't show up that night or the next day, everybody in
town turned out to hunt. They followed over that ridge and
way up into the ledges, then lost the tracks. Finally they gave
up, but they sure hated to lose that bear."

"There was a sawmill in this brook once; see that
stonework? The arch was the millrace. One time one of the
sawyers got killed. They asked one of his old friends to go to
the house and break the news. They knew he would be the
one to do it tactfully. So he went and knocked on the door,
and when the woman came, he shouted," — and here Fran
filled up his lungs and bawled — " 'YER HUSBAND'S GOT
HIMSELF SAWED IN TWO — HE'S REAL BAD — THERE'S BLOOD
SPLASHED ALL OVER THE MACHINERY!' "

Nobody can say I didn't get a good chance to look over
the town and hear all about it. Like Ma, I sized it up, and
married the local boy anyway.

ᵈ Cider Apples

MA WAS adept at getting value from her family, and, for that matter, from her "guests" as well. Fran was just as adept at manipulating tasks to derive the most entertainment for himself from them.

He phoned one evening suggesting I come to the farm early the next morning as the day's project was to take the horse and wagon and go to the cider mill, ". . . and bring some sandwiches . . ."

When I got there, breakfast was finished and Ma, voluminous in a white apron, was fussing over the bags of apples Fran had collected. The old apple trees in front of the house did not produce edible fruit. Their apples were wormy and wizened, their twisted, kinky branches stark against the mirror of the pond. In the spring they took turns having blossoms. Wayland had already hitched up the horse and was leaning silently in the doorway.

"Well, now, Fran," Ma was saying, "did you pick up all the apples? Have you enough burlap bags? Wayland can get those bushel baskets from the shed if you need 'em. He can just empty out the potatoes — "

"They're turnips," Mabel interjected.

Ma went on, "Those wasps didn't bother you, did they? The little boy who got stung made a terrible fuss. I told his mother to make a poultice with baking soda . . . Now, after you leave the mill, stop at the blacksmith's and pick up that bolt for the hayrake. Going to Sam's? Why? It'd be quicker if you went round by Cora's first — I want you to pick up those two broody hens she has shut up. They'll make good stew. Have we plenty of onions, Mabel?"

"One of those hens died," said Mabel.

"Oh no, it didn't . . . it was just lying down — "

"It's *dead!*" said Mabel fiercely. Ma ignored her.

"— and ask Cora for that piece of red wool she has; it'll go real good in my rug."

Finally we climbed aboard the wagon and rattled off at a spanking pace. Behind us, a window opened, and Mabel yelled something after us. "Can't hear you!" Fran hollered back as we bowled along.

Jim was one of the last working horses in the town, and Ma was devoted to him. The farm wasn't worth a tractor, but Jim could do it all. He was a spunky little Morgan, clever and, Ma claimed, "quick as a cat." She herself was a capable driver, and Wayland often hitched Jim to the buggy so that Ma could drive him to the village, either to take Mabel home or to go to the Ladies Aid. If she met a car, she held to the center of the road, and if the car was forced to take to the ditch, too bad for it. Cars were nothing but noisy pests anyway.

We dropped off our cargo of apples at the cider mill, but the mill owner shook his head. "Sorry, Francis, I'm real sorry. But my wife died this morning and I'm all shook up. Come around first thing tomorrow, and I'll git right at them."

Next, the blacksmith shop. Inside, Arnie the smith roared a greeting to Fran, who stepped down to hitch the horse. I stayed in the wagon as Fran said it would take only a minute to pick up the bolt. In fact, he was gone some time, and I was left to inhale the acrid stench of singed hooves. (Ah, where are the smells of yesteryear?)

As Fran came back out, the blacksmith stood watching us leave, minus the bolt, of course, which he hadn't been able to find. Arnie was scowling and didn't return our farewells.

"What was the matter with him all of a sudden?" I asked. "It can't be me, he hardly knows me — it must be you. What did you say?"

"Nothing much. Oh, I know! I just asked if he had seen

Willy lately. Willy was in our class at school. And that must have reminded him of that day, in fourth grade, I think, when we sat side by side and were both terrible. Whenever the teacher had her back turned at the blackboard, we would make rude noises. And this day, she whirled suddenly and cracked Arnie over the head with the spelling book — not me, just him! It knocked tears out of his eyes. He'd always been the biggest, the loudest of us all, and now, tears! In front of the whole school! He still holds it against me if he is reminded of it."

Our last stop was at Cora's, where over cups of strong tea and wedges of gingerbread, Morris, Cora's husband, gave a long-winded, horrendous rundown of the boil on his neck.

We brought back no cider, no bolt for the hayrake, the two broody hens had died, and the red wool had been used as a pad for Cora's ironing board. Still, it had been a satisfying day. For the first time I had felt comfortable meeting the people Fran had grown up with. With Fran there, I wasn't made to feel an outsider by the "born-right-here-on-the-land" natives.

ᛦ Sam

THE CIDER mill was on the road to Sam Mason's, so when we went to pick up the cider the next day, we did stop off to see Sam. Fran tied Jim up in the barn, and we went in to share our lunch with Sam, that is, as much as he would accept.

"What's this, lettuce? Well, no thanks, got no use for it. Now I just might take one of those eggs if they ain't all doctored up."

Sam was a one-man institution. He lived alone in a vast Victorian house. It was bleak and unobliging; no woman had ever laid a finger on its interior. There were no curtains, no tasteful rugs, no potted plants, no style, just sheer bachelor perfection. The kitchen had a stove, an oilcloth-covered table and Sam in his rocking chair, comfortable and jovial.

He was stout, rosy and bald. His wheezy chuckle started high up by his gold collar button, and rippled down the round red slope of his suspenders. He made a living building cottages for the summer people. He became their caretaker, patriarch and fount of local lore. Indispensable to their comfort, he was cottoned-up-to, cherished and spoiled.

Summer people were sensitive about the cool gap existing between them and the rooted families of the town. It wasn't that they were cut off from the local scene, it was that they could never get in at all. No one but Sam took them in. He was the only one who laughed not at them, but with them. They would have liked to adopt him, to show him off to their friends as a local "character" and thus imply that they had some footing among the local people. But here Sam drew the line. He wouldn't be shown off nor would he come to their houses for dinner. He would have no part of their social life. If they wanted his company, they were welcome to it, in his own house, on his terms. They could come to him at any time, but he wouldn't budge a foot.

College-age sons of his summer people made Sam their own. There was a warren of unfurnished rooms upstairs in his house, and there they flocked, given an open invitation to use the place as a haven from the rigors of campus life.

For Sam, the college boys provided more entertainment than the radio. In the fall and winter they would come on the spur of the moment, bringing their food, their bedrolls, their girls, their exuberant muscles. In the evenings, starting at five o'clock, Sam would play host, rocking in his chair, promoting discussions, making teasing insinuations about their love affairs. He enjoyed stirring up a bit of trouble here and there. But this atmosphere of loose joviality was a one-way street. Sam had a core of native reserve, and his personal life was off-limits as were any suggestions for improvements to his household. Tools were sacred.

One weekend a group of Harvard med school students blew in, led by an athlete named Paul. They were bursting with vitality. Sam's kitchen was swamped with sacks and cartons, with brown bags sprouting greens. Every chair and table overflowed with supplies. Sam sat in his chair, observant and imperturbable.

Eager to get outside and climb Mount Monadnock, they banged about, explaining to Sam that they had a super dinner all planned and would be back in plenty of time to get it ready.

"Don't do a thing, Sam; it's as good as done now," said Paul, as he pulled a huge turkey from its wrappings and flung it on the table. Seizing an axe that stood in a corner of the kitchen, he proceeded to chop wood for the stove on the doorstep. The doorstep was granite. The axe was Sam's.

Sam watched, rocking back and forth and saying nothing. Laden with wood, Paul came back in, stoked the stove, and popped the turkey into the oven. Beaming, he called, "All ready, gang? We're off to build us a man-sized appetite."

Just as he was going out the door, Paul turned back and said, "We'll be back by five, Sam, maybe sooner. Keep an eye on the turkey, will you?" He charged off, his fuse sparking with energy.

When they returned, Sam was still sitting in his rocker reading the paper, apparently unmindful of the thick black smoke choking the kitchen. In one giant step, Paul wrenched open the oven door.

"Sam!" he howled, "I thought I asked you to watch the turkey!"

"I did," said Sam. "I watched it."

While the turkey was being scraped free of its black crust, Sam took the axe out to the barn, where he kept his grindstone, and removed the nicks. Later, he took the offending woodchopper aside and said mildly, "Paul, I like you fine; you're a real good young feller. But I don't like a damn thing you do."

Ma and Sam never met. Eight miles apart, they kept their distance although both were sociable people and shared the same philosophy. Either would have welcomed the other to his house, but neither wanted to be the guest. It was a case of the Mountain and Mahomet, but which was which?

Sam was older than Ma, and by the time his medical students had become full-fledged doctors, he had aged and found it difficult to cope with the ebullience of his youthful followers. They sensed this, and more and more often, as Fran and Newt went back and forth between Sam's and Tolman Pond, the young people gravitated to Ma's place, finding there the same gamy flavor and rich compost of personality that had brought them to Nelson in the first place.

A year or so after Fran and I were married, Sam began to fail. He sent word that he would like Fran and me to come over. When we got there, he confided his problem, namely that he was being overwhelmed by loving attention from his anxious friends, stifled by suggestions, overloaded with nourishing hot soups and casseroles. After a lot of preliminary waffling, he came out with it — would we consider moving in with him? That, he said, would silence all those who were insisting that he should no longer live alone. We were taken aback. We had just finished building our house and were contemplating producing a baby. It was embarrassing. We were flattered — but why us? We could think of other young couples who would jump at the chance. Finally we wormed it out of him.

"Well, now, it's like this," Sam said. He thumbed towards me. "She's the only woman I know, the only one I can count on, who wouldn't try and make me eat fresh vegetables."

(Put it on my gravestone.)

❧ Don't Fence Me Out

OFTEN I rode alone. As Ma's all-purpose handyman, Fran couldn't always steal time from the farm chores to ride. On those days, I would jog contentedly along the old roads that Fran had introduced me to. There were no grandiose inspiring views. If I had ever had a romantic picture of the quaint beauty of rural life, I might have been disillusioned by the slipshod reality. Perversely, I became attached to it.

My horse browsed from bush to bush. I let the reins hang any old way, I dozed, I daydreamed. From horseback, the air had motion and life, unlike the air inside cars, those insulated mechanical containers. Clip-clopping along, the horse stirred up leafy odors, and the air breathed through me, infiltrating my bloodstream. I had time to dodge cobwebs strung from tree to tree, and to watch feathers drift in patternless flights.

As I slouched along, my eye would catch the sight of some decrepit farmhouse buried in a welter of lilacs. I would notice the old dog tied to his barrel, the lines of tatty laundry, and the pasture gates fashioned from rusty bedsteads. If that was a face at the window, whose was it? What was all that stuff on the porch — maybe a plush sofa with a cat or two — and was that black hump an old cooking pot, or was it a nesting hen?

Vines hid everything. It was all very mysterious and inviting to my inquisitive eye. As I passed, I would tidy it all up in my mind to meet the suburban standards ingrained in me. The fence needed straightening (before summer people, there wasn't a straight stone wall in all New England), and would the grey, weathered boards be better off with a fresh coat of yellow paint, or white with green shutters? How about carriage lamps by the front door? Before I was out of sight of that farmhouse, I would have mentally metamorphosed it into a town house in the suburban New Jersey I had never much cared for.

Once or twice, partly out of nosiness and partly out of a wistful hope of striking up an acquaintance, I would stop to ask for a glass of water from the woman in the house. This was always brought to me courteously, outside, her body in the doorway blocking my sneaky eyes. Then, taking the glass, she would retreat inside. She didn't slam the door, nothing so crude, and didn't need to; her attitude made the message clear. "You're a stranger — stay on your side of the fence, and I'll keep to mine."

If Fran was along, things were very different. He was at home with everyone, he spoke their language, he had been to the same school, sat next to them at Town Meeting. We'd not only get water, but be offered cider, or perhaps some newly made rhubarb sauce. But then, Fran was a native.

By managing to marry Fran, a smart move that took some doing, I thought I had it made. Now I would no longer be a Summer Person, but a Native. Better yet, perhaps, a crossbreed, at home on both sides of the fence.

Since this unseen barrier seemed flimsy, it was easy to underestimate how deeply rooted it was. Tactful, gentle pulls didn't budge that fence; yanks made no impression and kicking proved futile and painful. Some part stayed hidden down in the weeds ready to balk my good intentions.

Fran's family gave us a beautiful piece of land, a rise of

pasture behind their farmhouse. On it we built a house that was new and just "neat," if not quite up to the standards of the town I'd come from. Nothing was at right angles; there were no starchy maids, no immaculate lawns, no suburban rules of social life.

Our house was ideally located, out of reach and out of sight of the old folks, but within shouting distance, while they and their raggle-taggle barn and back yard were inescapably part of our view.

Like most of the other houses in the area, the farmhouse was comfortable, inviting, and bedraggled. For several generations, things had been left just where they'd been dropped, handy and easy to find, a constant challenge to my suburban urge to straighten up. Every time we went down for a meal or to pick up the mail, my busybody instincts went to work. I'd chase the hens off the doorstep and line up the muddy boots on the porch. I'd arrange everything side by side, all prunes and prisms. It was the wrong way to go about becoming a native. Fumble-footed, I was bound, sooner or later, to stub my toe on Ma.

As newlyweds, our design for living (if such a higgledy-piggledy batch of interests could be called a design) never included Ma's boarding house. We were to live independently, to one side. Nor was it ever suggested that I take part in the boarding-house life. If it had been, I would have withdrawn my shocked head into its shell and sulked. No boarding house for me. No indeed, we were to be independent, we were to live *on* the place, not *in* it.

Fran, however, was in and out of Ma's kitchen or in and out of the barn all the time. Whatever we needed always seemed to be in the other house. Saws, hammers, pails and kettles shuttled back and forth every day. Fran's was an in-and-out sort of life anyway, a flea market of interests. He made and sold pictorial signs for inns, he had a part-time job with the newly hatched *Yankee* magazine, he went to the House of Representatives every other year, he gave riding lessons, and he was called on for every type of emergency at the farm. He kept a busy foot dashing from one house to the other. The bustle of Ma's kitchen was in his blood.

But not in mine. After all, I was only a pseudo-Tolman, a transplant, occupied with bookbinding, trips to the city and, eventually, the care of a baby. I planned to keep my distance.

Neither Fran nor I had the knack, that miraculous knack, of making ends meet. So, right from the start, we never refused an invitation to dinner. Every day there we were, eating; we never missed. Ma's dinners were more than a fringe benefit — they were a lifeline.

At that time, Fran's brother Newt and his wife were quartered at the farmhouse and available as built-in help. Not until they separated, first from the farm and then from each other, leaving a gap in Ma's work force, did I get sucked in. Then, to pay our way, to show our appreciation for the dinners, we did a few dribs and drabs. Fran was handy with busted beds or chairs — he was good at patching up things — and I could make a bed or flick a dust rag about as well as the next person. Occasionally I'd get inspired and do a bit of mending or painting, but not often, as Ma just didn't notice things like that, and my efforts went unappreciated. Still, little by little, we trickled into Ma's orbit, drawn as much by the warmth, the gossip, the rackety goings-on as by the superb food.

CHAPTER TWO

❧ Mabel

BEFORE MA came into the kitchen in the morning, Wayland had already fetched Mabel from the village. Ma had gotten heavy and her knees hurt, so now she had to control her "staff" either from her stool or from her couch in the sitting room nearby. As a substitute for reliable legs, Mabel was indispensable. She was Ma's personal aide, her source of gossip and when Ma needed one, her scapegoat. If Ma herself could no longer get out to the garden to point out a neglected patch of carrots, she knew if one was there. Mabel's bright little eyes saw into every corner, and she reported back to Ma. Mabel was the right hand, even more so than Wayland, as she was always there in the kitchen, whereas Wayland had a way of disappearing out to the barn.

Mabel boiled about among the pots and pans, scatter-brained hair on every which way. She was built to last, solid and foursquare, and she should by rights have had a caster at each corner. Periodically hooting with laughter, red in the face with exertion, she rushed about obeying orders, but not instantly or unquestioningly. She was just as Yankee as Ma and not about to take an order without offering an obstructive comment. To whatever Ma demanded, Mabel raised a cackle of objections. Nevertheless, Ma's will got done.

"Mabel, fetch down that big brown bowl. No, not that

one, the one with the blue. Has the dough started to rise? Well then, set it on the back of the stove. I need a half cup of sugar, and will you call the butcher and tell him I didn't care for the way he cut that shoulder of lamb, tell him — No, I'll tell him myself when I get to it. Has that Mrs. Whosit stopped by for the recipe she wanted? Oh, Mabel, of course you know who I mean, what's her name, the woman with the red hair, well, not awfully red, kind of washed out. You know her name as well as I do. She wants that recipe for brown bread, the one from the *Globe*. Where is it, anyway? You put it somewhere — find it, will you?"

"You took that recipe up to the Ladies Aid and didn't bring it back," Mabel retorted, "and her hair isn't red. It's more grey, a pinkish grey. The bread's rising too fast; I'd better bring it over to you so you can punch it down."

"Does the stove need wood?" At this moment, a boarder came in from the dining room looking for a cup of coffee, and both women called out simultaneously, "LOOK OUT! Watch the stovepipe!" Too late. The boarder's head struck the overhead pipe, and it came crashing down in a cloud of soot.

"Mabel, quick, get Wayland! He must be in the barn — hurry!" Mabel thundered out and brought him back. While Ma fired directions that everyone ignored, the boarder pushed one end of the pipe back into the stove, Mabel supported the middle, and Wayland fitted his end into the chimney. It had happened before; they were schooled in their roles. Except for the boarder, who, though initially flustered, soon caught on to what needed to be done.

The stove was set out from the wall, and there was a passage behind it connecting one end of the house with the other. Going through this passageway, you were obliged to duck under the stovepipe, making a bobbing motion like an obeisance to royalty.

Ma turned to the boarder. "Well, now! That's fixed. Come right over here and sit down. We'll get you some coffee. Here's some warm johnnycake and some of my marmalade, made last winter. It's very tasty. I put some grapefruit rind in, adds just that extra tartness. Wayland, why don't you take his jacket outside and give it a good shake. Wasn't it lucky that you had brought the dough over here, Mabel. I threw my apron over it just in time, and there's hardly any soot, just this little bit on the top which'll wipe off all right."

Like a substantial and autocratic relative, the stove ruled the kitchen and demanded constant attention. Mabel had had years of catering to its crotchety whims. She fed it small, delicious scraps of kindling when it was chilly. She delicately tilted its lids when it was hot. She was an expert at handling it, and an expert at fending off Ma's suggestions.

"Mabel, open the damper more."

"Goodness, no! — it's open way too far already."

"You should have had someone empty the ashes this morning. Where's Wayland — WAYLAND!"

Flat-footed and choleric, Mabel was in spite of everything a very rare person. She was contented. She was happy with her home, a tarpaper shack with a lean-to to windward, and she was happy with her family, and especially with her husband, George, whom she quoted as an authority on every subject.

George had done nothing at all for years except "lining bees" (whatever that was), and he was an authority on that, too. In answer to the daily question of "How's George today?" Mabel always beamed and said, "Oh, George is just fine!" George had had both his legs amputated because he had had the poor judgement, after letting his feet freeze, to put them in the open oven without taking his boots off. Gangrene set in. The only complaint Mabel was ever heard to make of George was when she said, "Don't know what's come over George —

he won't stand up any more." After he got his new legs, she got over this petulance and took as good care of him as she did of her other precious possessions.

Mabel topped all statements. According to her, she had it all just a little bit better than anyone else. When Mrs. Gilsum came back from an auction, she went into the kitchen to have Ma pass on the value of her buy. Not that Ma was an expert on antiques, but she did have the air of one as she held the cut-glass celery dish in her floury hands and turned it about. From her position at the sink, Mabel eyed the dish sharply and announced, "I got one at home just like it. Only mine don't have a crack."

Mabel's ancestry was also unequaled. She pointed out on a shopping trip a fine Colonial house in Keene, graced by a fanlight over the door and a cupola on top. "My grandmother's uncle by her first marriage used to live there, but they moved out. There was mold in the cellar."

As for her antiques, her shack must have been twice as big on the inside as it appeared from the outside, but we could never prove this, as she didn't admit anyone past the door. When we went to pick her up, she was always ready and waiting, her square body blocking the view. She couldn't be put down, but we had to add great dashes of salt to her statements.

Then came the day Ralph Townsend came to open the October shooting season with Fran. As was his custom, he stopped in the kitchen to pay his respects to Ma and Mabel.

Ralph believed that life was for living and he was the man who knew how to do it, quite in the style of Henry the Eighth, only with fewer wives. He indulged in haunches of venison, trays of oysters on ice, bottles of imported wine. He went south for quail shooting, to Norway for salmon, to Switzerland or to the Andes for skiing. Wherever he went, he trailed retainers to wait on him so that the little things in life wouldn't hamper the big things. However, he did restrain his lavish tendencies at Tolman Pond, parking his dogs and guns in a trailer behind the house, careful not to trespass on Ma's domain. As usual, he brought Ma a suitable present — a basket of big, fat trout.

Mabel, sloshing dishes around in the sink, muttered, "My boy caught two in White's Pond a lot bigger than them." Ralph ignored this remark and continued telling Ma how he had come up by way of Winchester to hunt up his great-great-grandfather's grave.

Mabel said instantly, "My great-great-grandfather came from Winchester, too."

Ralph went on smoothly, "— and what's more, I not only located his gravestone, but found that the lettering was still perfectly legible. 'Myron J. Smith,' all in good shape."

At this point, Mabel exploded in a geyser of soapsuds. "My great-great-grandfather's name was Myron J. Smith, too!" In fact, their great-great-grandfathers were one and the same.

From then on, every time that Ralph came, as he walked into the kitchen, he would call out, "Hello, Ma! Hello, Cousin Mabel!" and Mabel would nearly burst her sides with satisfaction.

❧ The Kitchen

MA'S PLANTS were on a shelf in the sunny alcove off the kitchen in front of the house facing the pond. We had our noon meal there when she didn't have boarders to cope with. The shelf was over the window seat where we sat, and had been made particularly to suit the needs of the plants, for their comfort. They had the best light, the best sun and Ma's constant attention. Never mind that this shelf was so low that we had to scrunch down, our heads driven into our spines. Ma didn't notice as her loving eye was directed up to her plants. Each had been placed in her care so that her green thumb could do its job. They weren't boughten plants — heavens no — they were either leftovers from the garden or relics from summer people.

"Mabel, are you going to bring in the soup? Well, bring along that glass of water with the bay leaves soaking in it, the spider plant looks a bit peaky." It not only looked peaky, it looked mean and peaky. A drooping, whiny plant with a long, hairy string dangling a small scrofulous hand that reached down, down towards our heads. Beside it on the shelf was a venerable Christmas cactus, grey, hoary, and barren, producing no flowers at Christmas or any other time, although it had been dosed over the years with infusions of tea, with the nutritious scrapings from Wayland's crusty black pipe, with spirits of arnica, all to no avail. Its neighbor was tall, with stiff, cruel blades; if it fell it could crack a skull. Next to this was a surprise, a cheeky little begonia, pink and bursting with tiny flowers, each lasting only a day. The withered petals were tossed overboard, falling into the soup or onto our heads, but at least they didn't have legs. The next plant — ugh! It lived in a saucer in a brown bog, a wad of snarled fuzz sheltering a resident black beetle.

Then the day came when the cactus put out a bud.

"Mabel, just look at that! Now didn't I tell you that buttermilk would do the trick — !"

Mabel instantly retorted, "No, it never was the buttermilk, it was those soapsuds I doused it with."

Neither of these treatments worked for the spider plant; it remained as sour as ever.

Luckily for us, Ma never read the bulletin from the Department of Agriculture, which said that spider plants had been found efficacious in reducing air pollutants, especially formaldehyde used in building materials. Spider plants sucked it up as if it were champagne, and under the influence burst out in an ecstasy of growth. An illustration showed a plant with a head of hair to rival Tina Turner's, including multiple strands of dangling fingers.

But Ma never read the article. The next concoction she and Mabel worked on was made — judging from the smell — from the residue of boiled turnips. Perhaps formaldehyde wouldn't have been so bad after all.

The kitchen was an architectural nightmare. With five doors, two stoves (one for summer and one for winter), two sinks, one large red linoleum-covered table, *and* Ma and Mabel, there was little floor space left over. Luckily, once Ma was established on her stool, she was a permanent, noncirculating fixture, and Mabel worked around her. It was a perfectly timed, heavyweight pas de deux. Not graceful, but functional.

The two sinks were placed at right angles to and almost touching each other. The new one was a white enamel affair, its finish already showing wear where Mabel's stomach pressed it daily; the ancient soapstone sink had stood in its niche for a hundred years, ever since water was first piped in. Each sink had its own particular use and its own status. The new one was privileged to do the dinner dishes, while the old one was a catch-all for utensils left to soak, for the milk pails and separator, for dandelion greens to be washed or for fish that Wayland would clean sooner or later.

The old icebox had been built with the back opening into the shed so that ice blocks could be placed directly in it and not have to be carried, dripping, across the kitchen floor. Now that there was a new refrigerator, the door of the old icebox gaped open on shelves used to store a hodgepodge of egg boxes, paper bags and dried bunches of catnip or parsley.

The back of the kitchen had been extruded to make room so Ma could have a baking counter. If Wayland had extended the natural roofline to enlarge the space, Ma would have had to sit on the floor. Instead, the new roof had been raised and tipped up, forming a catch basin between the old and the new. Here, snow collected, causing the ceiling to sag as it melted. The ceiling drooped lower and lower — just one more obstacle, like the stovepipe. In wet weather, a row of pots and pans tried to take care of the dribbles, but splashes and rivulets still made winding paths across the uneven floor. These hazards were taken for granted on rainy days, but even on dry days the cats' dishes could be almost as hazardous. They were supposed to be lined up against the wall, but the cats always licked them out into the traffic pattern.

Ma was happiest in her little baking nook. From here she could oversee the woodshed, the chicken house and all the back-yard activity. She rolled out dough, smacking and pounding it, often singing hymns in loud and triumphant bursts. "Holy, Holy, HOLY. — Mabel, come here and see if that isn't a woodchuck headed towards the garden — Lord God ALMIGHTY — WAYLAND!"

The kitchen trapped everyone. It was noisy, unsanitary, cluttered, steamy, full of laughter, protests of outrage — a controlled hubble-bubble. No matter what was in preparation, everyone felt free to stop by and visit. Ma was a master at accepting greetings, absorbing gossip, all without losing her place in the cookbook. Everyone passing through made some contribution.

Ma squabbled with the Greek who came by every week with vegetables. They fought over every carrot, and every nickel. Sometimes, just to prove a point, he would take a stint at the stove. Using her black iron "spider," he showed Ma his own recipe for zucchini (olive oil, garlic and chopped walnuts).

The grain man wouldn't be allowed to leave until he settled an argument about last week's bill. "Mabel, find the receipt — look in that knitting bag behind the door." Ma did like having people underfoot.

There was one exception to this — Belle. Ma's stability and regal self-possession were legendary, but Belle could blow it all.

Belle's sporadic visits had begun early in the life of the boarding house. At first, she had arrived driving herself in a horse and buggy, the seat beside her piled with bundles, cartons of books, and bulging sacks, some tied with string to the stays of the buggy top. Wayland or Fran would help bring in her belongings, and then unhitch the horse and put it in an extra stall.

She came from a well-to-do, scholarly Boston family, who saw to it that as soon as she could lisp, Belle would be well versed in Latin and Greek. Crammed to bursting with culture, her brain had over the years developed cracks. Boston proved to be too confining for this charged mind, so her family had provided her with an outpost in Dublin, New Hampshire, where it was hoped she would find intellectual companionship. Why she also had another house on a back road in Nelson, just seven miles away from the Dublin house, was never clear. Tolman Pond was a way station between her two houses.

No sooner had she opened her Dublin house in the spring than she felt a simultaneous urge to open the one in Nelson as well, and, loading all her partially unpacked gear into the horse and buggy, she would set out in a beeline for Tolman Pond. (Some years she didn't show up, since her life included periodic trips to Europe in search of culture and intellectual stimulation. Although she was usually provided with a companion as a safeguard on her travels overseas, she was apt to forget the other's existence and had often left her caretaker stranded in some pension.)

She invariably came unannounced, by now via hired car rather than horse and carriage, and always managed to catch Ma off balance. The back yard, the barn and the pond were all within Ma's field of vision, but the front door was a blind spot. Before Ma had time to rally Mabel and head her off, Belle would suddenly be inside the house, bag and baggage, crying, "Sadie! I'm here!" as she tore open her bags and got to work with frantic speed, turning on the water in the downstairs bathroom full force and pitching armloads of winter clothes, accumulated laundry from weeks of travel, into the bathtub. In three minutes of frenetic action, Belle could destroy Ma's equilibrium and turn the ordered if rumpled kingdom of Tolman Pond into a shambles.

❧ Belle

WHEN HER things were soaking nicely, Belle would come into the kitchen, pull up a chair beside Ma's work table, and begin to fill Ma in on her latest trip.

She was a small, thin woman, with a mangled bun of white hair bristling with inadequate pins. Her face was never still; fans of wrinkles washed back and forth across it as she ended one nervous smile and started another. Her eyes snatched at Ma's face, dodged away, and went over the kitchen ceiling and shelves, over Mabel and the cats' dishes.

As she launched into a rapid statistical report on the condition of the Acropolis, Belle's hands were busy pushing bowls first one way, then another, fidgeting with the cookbook as she peeked into the back pages. Before long, Ma was adding three heaping spoonfuls of salt where she needed sugar, and Fannie Farmer was telling her how to make Mushroom Timbales aux Fines Herbes when she meant to make cottage pudding. When Belle jumped up to check on the bath water, Ma would mutter, "What under the sun was that all about? I couldn't make head or tail of it, and now I can't remember what we planned for a vegetable today, my mind is so upside down."

One year, Belle had come back from Greece on a Lord Byron kick. The boarders were subjected to endless recitals of "Childe Harold." They were equally unsettled by the way she would break open her baked potato and peer into its interior before deciding to take a bite and her habit of tearing her meat into tiny shreds and picking it over clinically. Until then, the boarders had enjoyed Ma's deep-fried fritters unequivocally, taking each mouthful in good faith, but doubt set in as they watched Belle attack *her* fritter.

It wasn't just food that was examined. Belle looked into everything. Over the next couple of days, as her clothes continued to soak, she would wander about, prying and peeking. In the living room, she took out books to look into the space behind. In the barn, she fiddled with bits of harness, opened up grain bins and peered inside. Moldy old bathing suits, mackinaws, ropes, anything hanging from a nail in the shed was taken down or pushed aside as she poked and hunted. All day she searched tirelessly, peeping into old paint cans, turning over boards. What was she after? If asked, she would laugh and turn her face away, looking upset.

Ma at her baking nook watched out the back window. "Why do you suppose she's moving that roll of chicken wire? I do hope she won't get her foot caught in the rat trap." The next moment, Belle had strolled away and was squatting down to examine the underside of a rhubarb leaf. Then she straightened up and moved off, holding her hand out for a dead frog that a boy had found.

"S-s-t, Mabel, quick — here's our chance!" Mabel, right on cue, let out a suppressed whoop, dried her hands on her apron, and started at a heavy trot for the bathroom. Dredging out a dripping armful of Belle's garments, she galloped out the back door and flung them over the clothesline, still unwashed. After this small, underhanded triumph, Ma and Mabel were overcome with the giggles.

As soon as she noticed that her clothes had gotten themselves dried, Belle summoned her hired car. Nervously bestowing an enormous tip on Mabel and a frenzied hug on Ma, she bundled herself off for her Nelson house, assuring Ma that she would stop by on her return trip to Dublin. She had forgotten to pay her bill.

With her departure, the family settled around the kitchen table indulging in deep breathing. "I'll send the bill to her bank in Boston. I've done it before and they always pay," said Ma. "I wonder if they'll think it odd if I add on something for the continuous use of the bathtub for forty-eight hours?"

"Nope," said Wayland, "they won't even question it."

Ma gave a little laugh. "You know, I can't help liking the old girl. I never know what she'll be up to next. I don't know whether to feel sorry for her or not. Something's worrying her, something she lost and can't remember what it is. I know how it frets *me* when Mabel loses things. But then, if she ever found what she is looking for, how would she know she had?" Ma sighed. "Mabel, get us some of those doughnut holes if there are any left. I always feel hungry after Belle leaves."

We sat in silence, Wayland preparing his pipe for a stint of smoldering, and the rest of us staring out towards the pond.

"Look at those butterflies," said Ma. "First they go one

way and the next second they flutter off. Why can't they make up their minds — they're just like Belle.

"Maybe it isn't a *thing* she's looking for, maybe it's an idea, a dream. Maybe she's looking for Spiritual Meaning, or What-Is-Life — or the Ultimate Truth . . . "

"Well," said Wayland, scratching a match with his horny thumbnail, "what beats me, if she's looking for the Ultimate Truth, what made her think she'd find it in one of my old fishing boots?"

A month later, Belle phoned Ma from Dublin. She apologized for not having come by on her way back, but she had been picked up by a relative and hadn't had the chance. She was calling, she said, to see whether Fran and I would come over that afternoon to select a wedding present from among the surplus furniture she had acquired during various expeditions. When Ma passed on this message, Fran instantly rejected it. "Oh, no, not on your life. You couldn't get me over there!"

But I wanted to go; we didn't have any chairs, and I couldn't see passing up this golden opportunity. Ma backed me up. "And be sure to take anything she offers. Whatever you can't use, I can." Fran was stubborn. He wanted to go fishing, but he was finally persuaded that we would get back in time for the evening rise.

When we arrived in our open-air Model A touring car, Belle was waiting for us. She brought us in through the back door to the kitchen, which looked as though seven maids with seven mops had recently been at work but had fled, leaving their mops on the floor. We picked our way through these, passing a large chamber pot which Belle kicked playfully, saying, "That's just for flowers, of course!"

By now, we were in the front hall, where there were a dozen old-fashioned studded trunks, all open and spewing forth their contents. One had croquet mallets and brocade curtains, a second held an intricately tooled sidesaddle, another had a feather boa writhing in a collection of boots, crocheted work and walking canes. A treasure trove where hours could have been spent window-shopping. (I wanted that sidesaddle.) But Belle led us right on through to the next room, where a jumble of tables were piled up like a café after closing hours. The room beyond had chairs — lots and lots of chairs. Some were facing each other, some were standing in another's lap. It looked as if a chair convention had just come to an end, and each had turned to argue with the chair behind it. Belle turned to us and said, "Now, what would you like? Pick out anything, I won't say a word. Now what would you think of this chair — or would you rather have a table?"

No, we said firmly, we needed a chair.

"Good," said Belle. "How would this one be?" She had her hand on a cerise velvet number, evidently a discard from some red-light district. "Or perhaps you'd find this one more suitable?" This was a Morris chair of cracked brown imitation leather.

"Oh, look!" I pointed to a small wooden chair in the center of the room. "That looks like just what we need."

Belle ignored me. "Do take a look at this one; it's extremely rare, it would be a handsome piece in your house." We were faced with a great carved wooden monstrosity, six feet high, a relic of the Nile, with broken gilded sphinx heads and studs of glass.

"I liked that little one."

"Of course, why don't you take it?" said Belle agreeably, "but just take a look at this. It has such a perfect shape." Its shape was perfect, all right, but there was too much of it, billowing out in busted curves, knobs and fringe.

Fran decided to call an end to all this. He fought his way

into the mob, picked up the little chair and brought it out held high over his head. He ignored Belle's next suggestion of the wicker chair with broken arms sprouting bamboo shoots.

Belle followed him out to the car, picking up a couple of Venetian glass bowls and setting them in the front seat. Fran put the chair in the back, where it fit perfectly.

"Oh, wait now, it might fall off!" Belle cried. "Just a minute while I get something to fasten it with." She scurried into the house.

"See," said Fran, "didn't I warn you?"

Belle came back with an armful of what turned out to be yards and yards of braid salvaged from some ancient couch, greenish brown and rotten. With this, she went to work in manic earnest, weaving strands all around the chair, in and out of the spindles, each strand breaking as she knotted and reknotted it. At last, Fran gently pulled her away from this spider web and started the car. "Oh, just one minute — I want you to have these," and she scuttled into the house and came back with three old Quimper plates. "Goodbye," she called. "Do come back tomorrow and pick out a table!"

Fran put the car in gear, and we eased away, leaving her looking small and alone, waving and smiling her jerky, anxious smile, one hand pushing her bun of hair back up to the top of her head. "What time do you think it is?" Fran asked. "It's getting dark; it'll be too late to fish."

Ma was delighted with the Venetian bowls, piling them with cottage cheese topped with a wreath of nasturtiums. The Quimper plates were just what she'd always wanted and just right for the browned water crackers she served with the soup (two cracker halves per person). The chair proved to be an antique Windsor, useful and sturdy — a real treasure.

By the time I managed to talk Fran into going back for a table, it was too late. Belle had returned to Boston.

The next summer, Belle made what was to be her final trip to France, to top up her classics, or perhaps to track down the Ultimate Truth. Right in the heart of the Bibliothèque Nationale, her overcrowded brain popped a valve. The story that eventually came back to Tolman Pond was that she had eluded her custodians and taken refuge in a cathedral. Here she barricaded herself behind bundles, paper bags, and a complete set of Lord Byron's works. Ma speculated that she must have been hard to dislodge, especially if she had set her heart on doing her laundry before she left.

◄◊ Headquarters

IN THE MIDDLE of the morning, confident that she had her organization in hand, Ma took a break. Leaning on her cane, she went into her sitting room adjoining the kitchen, still in sight and sound of everything that went on. She settled on her couch in a welter of cats, baskets and newspapers.

In her blond childhood, someone had once remarked that blue emphasized the blue of her eyes. From then on, blue it was. Her dresses were blue, the walls of her sitting room, her bedroom, pillows — everything — was sky-blue Pollyanna colored. Ma was no Pollyanna, though, and how her caustic nature survived this nauseating sea of blue was a mystery.

The sitting room was her office. Here she received her subjects, wrote letters, read the papers, curried the cats and played cards.

All evidence to the contrary, Ma was convinced that she was orderly and businesslike. Baskets were her filing system. She was surrounded by them. They held recipes, birthday and Christmas cards from years back, newspaper clippings, scraps of wool, dog-eared snapshots, bills, mending — each basket topped with a cat.

Next to her couch was an end table, almost hidden under its load of old magazines and her Bible, which she planned to finish reading someday. Another basket towered with old but still useful envelopes. Buried under there somewhere was a radio, a memorial to Amos and Andy and Fibber McGee and Molly, both great sources of entertainment in the past.

If Ma couldn't find something, she was shocked. It was Mabel's fault.

Once, a daring member of the family faced Ma with an ultimatum. "We're going to neaten up this room, and if you don't want all this stuff thrown out, you'd better check it over." Naturally, Ma was affronted, but after a while she settled down to the task and even began to enjoy herself.

She whacked a cat off the nearest basket and started picking out items, carrying on a running commentary to Mabel as she did so. Ma had a beautiful voice, clear and young, often full of laughter, and only occasionally (when speaking to Wayland, for instance) taking on a note of menace.

"Here's that card from Mary Gillis. I always did think she was a fool, but this picture of the kitten is sweet; I'll save it to show Alice. And Mabel, put two onions in the soup kettle. What is this brown stocking doing here? Oh, I see — it has a hole; where did you put the other one? Remind me to send Wayland for some darning cotton. And see if you can't find the mate to this, you must have put it somewhere. Have you got the milk on to warm? Well, put it on right away."

She unearthed a tousled ball of yellow wool, which she shoved back under, then came upon a bent pair of antique, wire-rimmed spectacles. "WAYLAND, come here and try these glasses. If they don't suit you, I'll give them to Alice." Some tattered recipes torn from a newspaper went into the pocket of her apron, and a few minutes later went back into the basket.

"Look, here's that jack of clubs we were trying to find all last winter! Mabel, where is that pack of cards with the red backs? How's that milk doing? For heaven's sake don't let it boil!"

The level in the baskets wasn't much lower after this effort, but at least the cats were more comfortable.

From her couch, Ma could see across the road through the branches of the two ancient apple trees to the pond. From another window, she viewed the barn yard, the kitchen garden, the hen swamp and the good-for-nothing hayfield that loafed up to a row of poplars at the far edge. She knew that where those trees fell away to a damp ring of alders, a woodcock lived. There in the spring he performed his mating dance, swelling out his chest, and selling himself with pompous and measured strut. Beep!, three paces, Beep!, and off he'd shoot into the air with rocket power. Here he became a fairy bird, fluttering and twisting at an immense height. Standing statue-still, one could barely see him, barely hear his thin, celestial song. Silence. Then he'd drop to the earth, settle his chin into his collar, and commence his amorous ritual all over again. Beep!

Ma couldn't see him from her sitting room, but she knew him. She kept track of all the wildlife on her property as well as the domestic animals — they were part of her domain. She knew the woodchucks, the occasional fox and anything else that crossed her boundaries. She knew who and what and where — her ears were very sensitive antennae. Each footstep was recognized, each shuffle or snuffle; not even a cat could tiptoe by. Wayland, with his rolling gait, his wheeze and his horrendous old pipe, didn't have a prayer.

"WAYLAND! Go take a look at my rhubarb. If there's a few stalks, say a dozen, I need them right away. And tell that boy to keep his bicycle off my grass! Fran, isn't that a woodchuck up there at the top of the field? DO something about it, for goodness sakes!"

Although there were times when she sat gazing contemplatively at the light on the pond, she was always ready for company. It was a mistake to think that she cherished solitude and wouldn't care to be interrupted. What really offended her was being overlooked, the feeling that she might be missing something. She liked to be the first to hear the latest.

Poor at remembering names, she had tried various memory-aid systems. One was by association, but this could trip her up. Mrs. Mason was called Mrs. Dixon. Mr. Morningside was called Mr. Nightshade. Her only reliable system was Mabel, and as someone approached, she would ask Mabel in a desperate undertone, "Here comes that Mrs. Castle . . brake? What's her name, Mabel — quick!"

"It's Cottleworth."

"Oh yes, of course, I remember now because it reminded me of — Oh, how do you do, Mrs. Cuttlefish? How nice to see you!"

Later she rebuked Mabel. "Why didn't you tell me her name was Cottleworth?" Ignoring Mabel's furious squall, she continued, "and didn't you think her dress was awful? With her shape she should know better than to wear pink; it blows her way up."

Ma planned meals in her head long before she came down to the kitchen in the morning. They were hidden away in her mind, and no one else had the blueprints. She didn't even confide in Mabel, and the result was often chaos. While breakfast was being served, dinner had to be started. These two overlapping operations didn't always mesh with well-oiled precision; the machinery was perpetually crossing itself up. Well-intentioned boarders coming in to lend a hand would often add another bit of gravel to the gears. Unlike a commercial hotel or inn, the boarding house recognized no gap between the guests and the hired help. Everything was integrated (or disintegrated), and there was no mystery about how things worked (or didn't).

❧ Cuisine

WHERE'S Wayland — WAYLAND, why haven't you brought in the milk? Have you separated the cream — there wasn't any? Well then, yesterday's cream will have to do. Mabel, put some in those two little white pitchers. Will there be enough beans for dinner? Wayland, go look in my garden, and never mind if they do seem a little tough . . . tough beans are good for the intestines.

"Mr. Crary wants two eggs for breakfast! Well, all right, *let* him have two eggs if that's what he wants — *two* eggs, imagine! We haven't two? What do you mean we haven't two? Of course we have. I remember seeing two eggs last night. Oh, well, yes . . . you're right, that one with the crack didn't look too good, now I recall I gave it to kitty. Mr. Crary shouldn't eat two eggs anyway, they're too rich for a man that eats so hearty." The business of the day was under way.

Ma was aware that the appearance of food was important; besides, she was proud of each dish and wished to present it as a creation. As on a cruise ship, platters were decorated with parsley or celery leaves or sprinkled with chives. Often this garnishing helped disguise the fact that a dish might be a little scant, but quality always made up for quantity.

Meals were ingenious and varied. Since no ingredients were bought in bulk, with the exception of sugar and flour, Ma couldn't have produced the same meal twice if she'd wanted to, and she didn't want to. There would have been little fun in that for a creative cook, and Ma managed to produce food that was consistently original and marvelously flavored.

Bread was basic. Never, but never, in all her years of cooking did Ma buy a loaf of store bread, and three times a week the house would be filled with the million-dollar smell of baking bread.

Soup was another basic. With no conscious effort, the kitchen was a recycling plant. All bones, vegetable bits, juices and tag-ends of greens automatically went into the soup kettle. After everything had boiled down, the strained-out residue went into the "hen's kettle." Dogs and cats got the plate scrapings. No attention was given as to what might be "good" for them; one day their diet would be mostly grease, and the next, bits of cake or old bread. If they were ever sick, they were smart enough to keep it to themselves; Ma wouldn't tolerate any nonsense from them.

Flavoring soup was one of Ma's talents. One could never figure out just what the flavor was — it was delicate and mysterious, rich and satisfying. She didn't believe in watering soup to stretch it, so a serving usually amounted to no more than a tantalizing half cup per person.

The flavor never seemed affected by the unfortunate location of the soup kettle, on the back of the stove just under a drying rack hung from the ceiling by wires. This was usually draped with damp dish towels, or a pair of Ma's stockings, or wet work gloves dangling from clothespins. If the boarders looked at this askance, they kept their mouths shut; they ate the soup.

Chowders were plentiful and hearty, made from corn, parsnips or, as most often, fish. In winter the fish was haddock, and Ma always gave instructions that the purchased fish must have "a good bright eye." Nobody else could detect any sparkle in a dead fish's eye, but Ma held staunchly to this impossible criterion. In summer, she counted on fish from the pond: perch, pickerel, hornpout or bass. Boarders were not only encouraged to fish, they were driven out. Ma considered all the fish in Tolman Pond to be hers by eminent domain. (Queen Victoria had rights over all the sturgeon caught in English waters.) Even tenants who rented a camp* were expected to check their catches with Ma.

Prince Pilsudski, an emigré and a newcomer to the farm who had probably never fished before in his life, caught by mischance a great, scrawny, buck-toothed pickerel. Astonished and triumphant, he paraded down the road toward the farm, stopping every few yards to show off his trophy. He showed it to Maria, an emaciated, buck-toothed woman who had a cottage and did her own cooking. It must have been apparent to him that this woman and his fish were meant for one another.

Ma, of course, had been apprised of his catch, and as soon as the prince entered the kitchen, she said, "I hear you caught a splendid fish. You can bring it in, and I'll have Wayland clean it right away so we can have it for supper."

"But Mrs. Tolman, I give him to Maria, she look so hongrey!"

"WHAT!"

Then, seeing how taken aback he was, she switched from outrage to kindly forgiveness. By the time he left the kitchen, Ma had persuaded him that Maria was only pretending to be thin, and that he had been conned. For the rest of his stay the prince made a valiant effort to catch a bigger, fatter, toothier fish to restore his place in Ma's esteem.

But Ma held it against Maria, and for some time after-

---

* New England for small cottage. Ed.

wards could be heard muttering to herself, "... *hongrey,*
indeed!"

She was skilled in making use of everyone. Any boarders
headed for Keene would be requested to keep an eye out for
some good celery, "say two bunches if the price is right, take
care that it is perfectly fresh and hasn't come from too far
away." If she saw someone setting out with a walking stick,
she called out, "Are you going by the west field? Here, take
this pail and if the blackberries are ripe, you can probably pick
a quart or two, and we can have Blackberry Goop tomorrow."

Blackberry Goop was a time-consuming treat made once
a summer. A whole pail of berries had to be smashed and
strained by Mabel, then strained at least twice more until
there wasn't a single seed left. By this time, Mabel was a
glorious color. The rich black juice was then cooked down
with just the right amount of cornstarch and sugar. The result
was a heady essence of late summer — rare, winey, delicious.

Cream was like gold; it was hoarded, especially when the
cows were going dry. Every drop was calculated for its ability
to enhance other flavors. A chowder might be short on lob-
ster, but the milk was creamy and loaded with potatoes and
onions.

Nearly all desserts had a quota of whipped cream. Ma was
a master at puddings; they were diverse and imaginative —
Indian meal pudding, Bavarian Cream, steamed chocolate
pudding, popovers with syrup, deep-fried balls of wholewheat
flour with nuts and maple syrup — each had its dab of
whipped cream. And somehow there had to be enough left
over to make the ritual Sunday ice cream. The freezer was set
in the barn doorway so the melting ice could dribble away
down the drive, and every boy on the place was drafted to
crank. Kibitzers stood about criticizing, needling and arguing
about who had done the most cranking and could by rights

lick the dasher. The end result was a small spoonful for each.

The milk — well, all the cream had been extracted. It was blue. A pitcher was left on the table to substantiate Ma's claim that "fresh milk" was always available. Children hated it, and it often smelled of cow. Later, it would be made into cottage cheese.

One winter when our son Barry was about ten, he shot a red squirrel. Ma, loth to discourage a future provider, cooked it. Luckily, there were no boarders, and we each got a piece about the size of a match or a toothpick. But there was plenty of squirrely flavored gravy poured over hot soda biscuits.

One of Ma's few critics was her own brother, Bill. After his wife died, he came to live at the farm. He was by nature a farmer and had hopes of cultivating a market garden on the farm property. He worked hard, but the soil defeated him, and he felt bitter and cheated. Bill kept comparing Ma's cooking to his late wife's, and grumbled about it when Ma was out of hearing.

"Gawd — just look at this." He lifted a knife-load of lemon meringue pie. "My wife could make a pie that was real stiff." He gave the knife a shake and the meringue plopped down on the plate. "Now, if I dropped my wife's pie, I can tell you it held together, it bounced, and that's the way I like my pie — real STIFF."

CHAPTER THREE

❧ *Front-Porch Sitting*

ON A SUNNY afternoon when the weather was fine, Ma liked to take her break out on the porch, where she would invariably be joined by an idle boarder or two, with Mabel on hand to field Ma's suggestions. In front was a patch of lawn, then the road, and then another patch of lawn and the pond. If there was no action on the road, there was the view of the Pond, its mesmerizing surface gleaming, both open and secret, often reflecting an imaginable heaven decorated with delicious puffs of clouds.

In summer, there was seldom any action on the road that twisted down the hill from Nelson. It was a poor road, steep and stony, but for this very reason it presented little danger to strolling boarders or their children; it had its own built-in safety system.

The approach from the top of the hill was wide and inviting, but as the road plunged downward, it rapidly narrowed to a trough, in summer alternately dark in shade or spotted with blinding shafts of sun. In winter the road turned black with deep and threatening ditches. Just attempting to inch out of the main rut could land a car in the boggy gutter.

Approaching automobiles were heralded by bangs and rattles. Small stones caught up by the tire treads would be thrown out against the underside of fenders to resound like steel drums. Large rocks, pushed up by spring thaws, cracked many a muffler, and cars could be heard groaning and whimpering some time before they hove into sight. Plenty of warning for sleeping dogs and children on bikes; even a turtle had time to move off the road.

Front-porch sitters became adept at identifying vehicles before they appeared. They learned from Ma.

"That must be Morris, sounds as if he was dragging a cutter-bar behind — why do you suppose he doesn't oil those wheels! Mabel, run out and see whether he'll be going back in an hour or so, he might be able to take Cora that catalogue I promised her . . . and Mabel! Don't stand there talking all day or we'll never get these peas shelled."

A few minutes later, after Morris and his cutter-bar had passed out of sight, the porch sitters jumped up and ran down to the road, as Ma cried, "Here comes the Mailman! Mabel, he should be bringing my Sears Roebuck order today — get down there quickly — it would be just like Edgar to go off without leaving it."

Mabel came back rubbing her ear as if it buzzed. "He said something like it wasn't 'forthcoming' — forthcoming? What in the world! Anyway, he didn't have it, and he kept hollering that you still owe him forty-two cents for the C.O.D. parcel he delivered last winter."

"Of course I don't owe him forty-two cents! I don't owe him a nickel and he knows it — just you go down and tell him that!" But Mabel balked. She knew it was a lost cause. Edgar had been stone deaf since he was a boy and traded on it. He wouldn't hear a thing he didn't want to, no matter how one yelled. And if he did choose to answer, it was with a vocabulary somewhere between archaic and dime-novel that left the questioner gaping or rubbing an ear in frustration.

Edgar had been mailman for years and knew the road

down the hill by heart, and yet even he had slipped off more than once.

There was the day when Fran, driving back from Nelson, came upon Edgar from behind at the top of the slope and saw that Edgar's car was weaving dangerously. It wasn't that he was going too fast; it was that Edgar was preoccupied with leading the Town Band — he was rehearsing it in his head. (Edgar not only played the cornet, but he was the Leader of the Harrisville Band.) Alone in his car, he sometimes got carried away by the spirited recitals he gave himself.

One hand on the steering wheel followed the wobbles of the roadbed; the other was beating time as Edgar's head wagged with the imaginary rhythm of the brasses. Fran honked in an effort to bring his attention back to the road. But just at that point Edgar flung his head back, raising both arms high, and vibrated his hands to a great drum roll, bringing the band to a glorious finale and his car into the ditch.

The car was canted in the mud at an alarming angle. Edgar struggled out and stood by despondently. Fran had a rope (he usually traveled with a rope, chains, a shovel and a suitable supply of bad language), and with some effort and in spite of Edgar's attempts to help, he managed to drag the car back onto the road without tipping it over. Overwhelmed with gratitude, Edgar reacted like an impresario. "Oh Froncis," he bawled tearfully, raising Fran's name to this emotional level, "Oh Froncis, I do thank you — you're a real sweetheart. I was right on the Ragged Edge of Despair!"

When the road provided no action, there was the pond to hold the attention of the porch brigade, the pond banded with emerald, a pool "dreaming deep." If no boys were thrashing about in boats, the pond's flat, shining surface might be broken by a breeze combing a pattern. That quick little V — was it a fish? a snorkeling turtle? Whenever a door was slammed, a dozen pollywogs leapt out of the water like tiny ballet dancers, then fell back in circular splashes. Then once more the pond would be a smooth, mirrored expanse, reflecting the lazy summer afternoon.

Front-porch sitting typified a boarding-house vacation — a vacation free of trips to the supermarket, free of appointments at the hairdresser's, free of repetitive chores and, best of all, free of nagging daily decisions. Ma, the benevolent queen mother, took care of it all; that was her role.

On either side of the porch steps grew an unidentifiable jungle. One plant, referred to by Ma as "my old-fashioned rose," was a sprawling, raggle-tail bush draped over a rusty frame of galvanized pipe. Beneath it, other plants struggled for survival, many of them clearly at death's door. But there was one that, for no good reason, was thriving.

Helen, lean and earnest, was a woman who came summer after summer, trying to figure out why she had come the year before. Tolman Pond baffled her; what drew her back? She yearned to resolve the puzzle. The pieces were all there lying about in disorder; if she could only put them together, perhaps it might make sense. She determined to go about this systematically, to file the parts, arrange things in categories and work it out. She asked sensible questions and noted the answers; she inquired why things were where they were and what for. But there was always something that eluded her.

"Is that a Red Trillium there by the lilac?"

"That? No, that's a Stinkin' Benjamin."

"Well, what's this one here by the step? It looks just like an asparagus . . ."

Ma leaned forward in her rocker to get a good look. "Yes, that's my asparagus — seems to be coming along just fine this year."

Helen eyed it dubiously. "Then it's a vegetable. Wouldn't

you like me to transplant it to the vegetable garden? I'd be glad to do that for you."

"Transplant it? Well, no," Ma said. "It seems to suit it right there, and I can keep an eye on it. Besides, it's pretty." Helen sighed and looked across the road to the patch of grass where a number of bent croquet wickets were indifferently lined up. Ma followed her gaze and remarked, "When I was first married we used to play tennis there. And balls would go in the lake all the time, you know. We'd wait till no one was looking, then take off our shoes and stockings, hitch our skirts right up to our knees, and wade in and screech! — how we screeched, trying to fish out those balls, scared we'd step on a frog."

Helen stared solemnly and said, "Why doesn't anybody line up those wickets so a ball could go through them, I wonder . . . ?" Nobody answered.

At the very end of her stay, Helen made a breakthrough — not a final solution to Tolman Pond by any means, but she did get hold of one spectacular fact — something she could bottle up and put on a shelf. She was so elated no one had the heart to disillusion her.

Like the other boarders, she visited with everyone up and down the road, but Helen made little attempt to remember names. She certainly didn't know by name the neighbors called Partridge. The day she was leaving, when her suitcase was already in the car, she went to say goodbye to Ma and came bouncing out, starry-eyed.

"Ma just told me the most amazing thing — every day while I've been here I've learned something new about Nature! And just now Ma told me that partridges catch fish! I can hardly wait to get back and tell my Bird Watcher's club — imagine, a partridge diving for a ten-inch pickerel! It makes the whole summer seem worthwhile."

❧ The Ones That Got Away

FAMILIES who stayed at the farm long enough finally got the hang of it and became Ma's regulars, but those who came with preconceived expectations often felt let down. They looked at the sagging roof line, at Ma's chaotic kitchen, and left, dismayed and instantly forgotten. There were some, like Helen, who came not knowing what to expect and never quite felt at ease, but still kept coming back for more. Some came by mistake, like the girl from Brooklyn, New York, who couldn't read a road map to save her life, and though bound for the Catskills found herself in Nelson, New Hampshire. Distressed and irresolute, she stayed on.

"Anyone want to go to the store?" I was on my way to Harrisville at noon in my Model A coupe, and stopped in front of the porch.

The girl from Brooklyn jumped down the steps and called, "I do. I need lots of things." Her long, dyed-red hair didn't begin to cover either her magenta bikini or the exposed areas of blue-white flesh.

"You'll be chilly," I warned. "My car has drafts." She ran into the house and came back wearing a long man's shirt, unbuttoned, of course. At the store, the mill hands were out in full force and enjoyed the treat she provided as she wandered up and down the aisles selecting Crackerjack, candy bars and comic books.

Coming home, she gazed at the dusty roadside bushes and, breaking open a Milky Way, said in a dreamy voice as she threw the wrapper out the car window, "You really got it made here, don't you? I guess it isn't so bad once you get used to it, all this simplicity and nature and stuff." She took a big bite. "Makes you think, kind of, how you can get along anywhere if you have to." She chewed for a while. "Anybody could hack it, y'know — as long as they have a philosophy, sort of. After all, all you really need in this world is the love of God and some first-class jewelry."

With this formula to sustain her, she did spend her vacation at the farm, but somewhere it must have failed her. When she left, it was for good.

One pleasant afternoon I sat on the porch steps watching the turtles sunning themselves on an old log that stuck up out of the pond. They looked contented, but it was hard to be sure — turtles never smile.

All was quiet, no one was around. Wayland had taken Ma and Mabel up to the Ladies Aid. Al, chore boy for the summer, was mending a roof on a camp well up the hill behind the farm. I could hear his rhythmic hammering.

A car drove up, stopped, and two women got out and walked up to the house. They were well-dressed, crepe-de-chine-type ladies — pearls, hats, matching handbags. They asked for Ma, and I explained that she was out and that I was substituting for her. After introducing themselves, one of them said, "We're looking for somewhere to spend a week or two this summer. Mrs. Charles Wentworth of the Dublin Garden Club suggested that we drive over and see your place."

"That's fine." I was all cordiality, the perfect summer-inn hostess. "You'll want to look around. Come right up and I'll show you the living room."

They came up the steps and started to cross the porch when all of a sudden there was a crack and a fearsome crash. A board had given way, and down went one of the women, one leg through the porch floor. She gave a frightened cry, one leg out of sight and the other doubled up under a voluminous spread of black-and-white silk. By some miracle she wasn't hurt, but badly jolted, in shock. Her friend and I tried to haul her up, but it was apparent that we were pulling her leg against the splintered edges of the boards. Something else had to be done; I was desperate. Leaving her to her friend, who was quacking in dismay, I dashed around to the back of the farmhouse and yelled for Al, whom I could still hear hammering away.

"AL! AL! Come down here, right away!"

The hammering stopped. "What?"

"Al, come on down right away, and BRING YOUR SAW."

"What did you say?"

I bellowed, lungs bursting, "AL — you come down IMMEDIATELY!"

"What for?"

I drew a deep breath and bawled, "YOU COME HERE! THERE'S A WOMAN CAUGHT IN THE PORCH — ."

Silence. Complete silence. The hammering didn't start up.

I rushed around to the front. I must do something, get the poor woman a glass of water, pour whiskey on her, do *something*.

Just then I heard Al. He came warily around the corner, took a look and made as if to bolt. But I was too quick for him and had him by the arm. "Now, you get at it," I snarled, "saw her out." He looked agonized, but seeing no escape, he approached with caution and gingerly pushed the silk skirt to one side. With me patting him reassuringly as though he were a nervous horse, he got the saw down a crack and went to work. I held the skirt close to the poor lady's body so he wouldn't have to face her large white thigh. Sweat dripped off the end of his nose, but I managed to keep the silk out of the way.

All this time the woman remained heroically calm, dignified, silent. One felt that this was the way she would have behaved on the deck of the *Titanic* as it sank beneath her feet. Her friend, on the other hand, jabbered enough for both.

Finally Al broke out a board. We ripped out another and, all hands together, we hauled her up.

Not a scratch! Not even a ladder in her stocking. She stood there, breathing slowly, reassembling her parts. She adjusted her corset, counted her legs, and checked her pearls with a steady hand. Ignoring Al and me, she turned to her friend and said with composure, "Eloise, my dear, I don't think this is exactly the kind of place we had in mind, do you . . . ?" They turned slightly towards us, bowed formally and left, walking with measured, sedate steps.

ᔒ Wayland

ACTUALLY connected to the house, the barn nevertheless kept its distance from it, being separated by an area which once had been a shed but was now an all-purpose room with a brick floor and a Ping-Pong table used by Wayland to dissect fowls, or to leave pails on or corn to be shucked. The cow-odorous barn was a refuge for Wayland, Newt, Fran and male boarders, a masculine version of the front porch. Here they gossiped, swatted flies and laughed as kids playing in the dust ducked in terror of the dive-bombing swallows. From the tall opening of the barn door they could observe the occasional circling osprey and bet on its chances of getting a fish. They too, like the front-porch sitters, checked out who came down the road and with what and made suitable commentaries. They exchanged sly, inside jokes, taking care to choke off loud guffaws; no one wanted to attract Ma's attention.

Here Wayland was a fixture, always there just before milking time. Brown and square, he leaned cross-legged against the barn door, a stance he had developed over the years so that, by shifting his weight to both feet, he could, at a moment's notice, appear to be about to do something, go somewhere, be right on the job. The danger over, he could lean back again at ease and tend his pipe.

He was in position the day a man drove up with a boy, got out and came up to him.

"Wayland — do you remember me? I'm Lucius — we used to come here years ago when I was a kid — and this is my son, Sammy. I was telling him about the time I caught the biggest bass of the whole summer, a giant — my gosh, that was some fish! You put it on a board and drew around it, remember?"

Wayland took his pipe out of his mouth and said cautiously, "Well, yes — I guess I do."

"And then you put that board up on a beam — it was a record fish. It might still be here, and I'd like to show it to my boy!"

"Now, let's see, seems as if it would be around — would that be it just under the hayloft? You can reach it if you stand on that crate."

"*That* little board? That can't be the one; isn't there another? Shucks! The date's right on it. I could have sworn it was twice as large." He looked at it abashed.

Wayland, an old hand at face-saving, said in his lazy, kindly voice, "Well now — that was some twelve years ago, wasn't it. Now then, you know how a fish shrinks out of water, don't you? Let's see now, in twelve years, counting shrinkage at, say, an inch a year — that must have been a *mighty* big bass." The man left, half-convinced, glaring at the pond as though it were to blame.

If Wayland had not had inner defenses, Ma would have brought him to his knees years before. But he never lost his quiet air of ownership, his whimsical self-esteem. A sense of humor, mental laziness and, especially, his deep devotion to Ma kept him impervious to her slings and arrows. One of his resources was his deafness, which he used for all it was worth; another was an ability on occasion to turn the tables on her.

There was the day in early spring — very early spring, still half winter — when Wayland brought in his annual bouquet of arbutus. He had a secret garden somewhere deep in the woods across the pond, which he had discovered and was his alone. Here, by scraping off a layer of wet, half-frozen dead leaves, he uncovered a hidden treasure of mayflowers and brought them in to Ma in his horny, calloused hands.

They were now on the kitchen table in a wide, shallow dish. Each elegant cluster had a pair of coarse, scarred leaves attached. Each cluster was turned out in pink and white, Easter-fresh. Ma pulled the dish to her and put her face down into the chill, clean flowers, breathing in the essence of spring, its fragrance, its hope. Sighing, she pushed the dish back to the center of the table and picked up her box of garden seeds, fingering the envelopes restlessly. She looked at Wayland sitting there in peace, relaxed, filling his old black pipe. Slowly and carefully, he tamped down a pinch of Prince Albert, added more, tamped that down, examined the bowl, and added just one more pinch.

As he reached into the box of wooden matches, Ma said impatiently, hoping to goad him into some form of early-spring action, "Wayland, how did you find things up at the Shaw camp? Was everything in order?"

"It was pretty good." He struck his first match.

"What do you mean, 'pretty good'? Were there any pipes broken? I thought I told you — "

"Yep. You told me. The pipes are OK." He pulled hard on his pipe without result, and reached for another match. "There was just one little thing. Last fall after everybody had gone, I fixed up the privy. I fixed it up real good." His pipe was drawing and he puffed out a cloud.

"Well, now — it seems a porcupine got in there during the winter and he ate out the whole dad-blamed seat — you never saw anything like it. He ate the hole into a *perfect square.* Didn't have a measure with me at the time, but I figure it's roughly eighteen inches both ways." He stopped to fumble for another match; his pipe had gone out. "But I didn't worry because," — he turned to look directly at Ma — "because I knew you'd be able to find a boarder that was just the right size and shape." His match burst into triumphant flame.

Yankee custom (and Ma) had him up at dawn, and by the time he got to breakfast, he had inched his way through a mountain of chores. By early summer, when the first of the regular summer people showed up, he'd have mended the worst of the leaky roofs, replaced some of the broken boards on the dock and shored up porches well enough to get by.

To a family coming to start their vacation in early summer, it was a relief to see that things seemed to be just as they had been when they left in the fall. The dirt road in front of the farm still hadn't been blacktopped (a perpetual threat from the Selectmen), the old hollow-trunked apple tree had survived yet another winter, and yes — Wayland was right there in the barn doorway. The world had been spitting and fuming all the past year, houses had been blown up, the earth had been shaken, but Wayland and the old apple tree had held their own, their roots undisturbed.

Right then, at that moment, the new arrivals would pull the mental switch breaking their connection with city life.

After unloading their gear, a first inspection showed that the camp was clean and in order, but a second check might send a child hot-footing it down to the barn. Wayland was ready, knowing it was inevitable; he knew that it was only at first glance that all seemed in perfect shape. He knew only too well that there was many a kicker lurking behind the scene.

"Mother says come quick — there's a rat up on the rafters!" (Or it might be a rattlesnake under the refrigerator.)

Wayland listened. He took out his pipe and examined it to see if it was drawing well. His face might have been a nicely baked brown potato for all the emotion this alarming news evoked.

"Well, now — seems as if we should be able to do something about that, doesn't it?" He pushed his cap back and scratched his head. "I could shoot it, but you know a rifle blows a real big hole through the roof. And if I used a shotgun, it'd make a gosh-awful mess. Tell you what, just as soon as I get through with the milking, I'll be right up and take care of it."

In any emergency, have no fear — Wayland would take care of it . . . *after* the milking. Milking was his escape hatch; it was always due at some time or other, and it gave a breathing space to let problems solve themselves. And sure enough, when he sauntered up to the camp a couple of hours later, the red squirrel had stopped behaving like a rat and retired to a tree. Or if the rattlesnake was the difficulty, he would probe under the refrigerator with a broom and then announce that the motor had a nature like a rattlesnake; the noise was quite normal. Now, he said, if it should stop rattling, that would be a bad sign, or if the refrigerator rocked back and forth, that might be bad, too — but that little rattle was a sign that the motor was in good health.

He took camp problems in his stride, though "stride" is a

poor description of his gait. He seldom did anything, but the way he didn't do it was reassuring. His value wasn't in speed, but in his square, comforting, earthy presence.

·ò Exotic Flavors

THE BOARDER in the barn doorway was squatted down on his heels, picking fishhooks out of a mess of tangled fishline. Fran, sitting on an overturned pail, had the reel in his hand. He tested the ratchet with his thumb, listening to the sound of it sing. Cross-legged against the door, Wayland was in position, idly watching Gigi, five-year-old femme fatale, come skipping down the road, short pink skirts bouncing and tiny patent-leather slippers kicking up the dust. Instead of heading for Ma and the kitchen, she shyly approached the barn-door group.

"Hi, Gigi, what's up with you?" asked Wayland. For a minute she just stood there, finger to her mouth, and then, raising her long black lashes, she studied each male in turn. Finally concentrating on Wayland, she lisped, "Mama say, she need a man."

All showed immediate interest. Fran set the reel down carefully, the boarder hoisted himself upright and Wayland shifted his weight to both feet.

"What did she say she needed a man for, Gigi?" Gigi lowered her lashes, raised them with studied art, and dimpling seductively, she whispered in a wistful little voice, "She say, zee toilet, she is br-r-r-oke."

Fran was up in a flash, and he and the boarder were off and away before Wayland could roll into motion. No toilet ever received more assiduous attention. Crowding into the camp, stimulated by glimpses of black lace and fluttering

Gallic charm and by heady French perfume, they somehow managed to extract a small trout from the intake pipe.

Gigi's mother was one of an influx of Europeans who found their way to Tolman Pond during the war. To the regulars, the strangers were a disconcerting interruption of the usual slow and easy summer life, but to the Tolmans themselves, the foreigners were a treat. New colors, new customs, new flavors. Without moving a foot away from home, the family was being afforded a taste of Continental life. It was mind-expanding, exhilarating.

Madeleine (Gigi's mother) and her sister Jacqueline were both refugees from Brussels. Madeleine's town house was, she said, "a mess with German ossifers." Her husband was isolated on their coffee plantation in the Congo, and Jacqueline's husband was in the Royal Air Force in England. Both were devoted wives, and their husbands were never far from their thoughts. Still, perhaps to keep their charms in good working order towards the day their husbands would return, both practiced diligently on whatever male material came to hand.

Their cottage was close to the pond, and their French voices would drift across the water, high and musical, lyrical notes in flight.

Seductive, enchanting, self-centered, they had one sure-fire *modus operandi* for extracting help from men (Gigi had it down pat): the low, inviting laugh, the musky hint of an exotic fragrance and the slowly lifted lashes. Predictably, it worked at Tolman Pond.

Wives became conscious of bulges in their hitherto comfortable slacks; they felt dowdy — either too flat or too fat. They sulked. Their children all seemed crude, ill-mannered and grubby in comparison with Gigi. It was natural that resentment should flare when Madeleine kindly offered to give these already touchy ladies Gallic pointers on sex appeal. In the nick of time, just before cracked egos could break into open wounds, fate took a hand. Or if not fate, then whatever saint it is that pops up in the aid of dowdy wives faced with rampant glamour.

A distinctly unromantic malady brought the two charmers crashing down to an everyday level. Now roles were reversed; the wives got in their innings, offering with vengeful generosity advice from their various stores of housewifely expertise. This advice was so plentiful and so contradictory that Madeleine and Jacqueline at length decided to take their Problem to the Top — in other words, to Ma.

A cat on her lap, Ma was sitting on her stool in the kitchen, supervising Mabel as she worked on a tower of pots and pans. She listened to their symptoms with interest, and agreed that they had come to the right place. Quite frankly, she said, she had put in years of research and was an authority; yes, indeed, she had the perfect cure.

"Well, now — we can certainly handle this problem. Mabel, show them our new batch of TNT." From its place on the shelf beside the catsup and mustard, Mabel brought out a jar. The contents were black and viscous, a tarry substance in which lurked dark shapes. Ma explained.

"It's my own special mixture. Just between ourselves we call it TNT — but it's really a compote of prunes with many other powerful ingredients added. Take some with you and try it. I guarantee it won't fail; you'll be *real* surprised."

Both women backed hastily towards the door, clutching each other. In trembling voices they cried, "*Mais non — merci bien, Madame — mais NON!*"

Retreating, the two intuitively realized they would have to go about finding a suitable cure by their own means, in their own tried-and-true way. So before long, one husband found that he had been seduced into lending his car, and another somehow promised his gas ration points. Now the two fragile, helpless little women headed for the bright lights of a civilized drugstore.

The first stop was Harrisville, but alas in the way of medicine for their delicate systems, there was "nutting." So they went on to Dublin — still "nutting, nutting at all. So we go on to Peterborough — ah! We find wot is *merveilleux*, *épatant!* Chocolate, you know — the Exlax ... ? We eat, we eat, all day we eat, we cannot stop, but" — here they both groaned, rolling tragic eyes — "but, *wot* a night ... *incroyable.*"

While the two beauties were thus hors de combat, complexions more green than creamy, antagonism went underground; now they were no longer dangerous. Meeting at the mailbox in the morning, the wives kept each other posted.

"I do feel sorry for Jacqueline, she has a pimple coming, quite a horrible one. Perhaps a little plain boiled custard would do her good. I'll make some this afternoon."

Oh, they were very, very kind and very, very thoughtful.

"Here's a letter from Belgium, I'll take it to Madeleine; perhaps it'll cheer her up, she's been looking positively yellow. I wouldn't be surprised if it isn't that awful coffee with chicory that she drinks all day. I'm going to tell her she's ruining her skin."

The tables were turned with a vengeance. Racked by internal upheavals, the French *femmes fatales* accepted suggestions so meekly that the cold war petered out. Two of the younger women went so far as to try out Jacqueline's eye shadow, and experimented with dashes of "Nuit d'Amour" at the Saturday night square dance. And Gigi, left to the care of the Tolman brats, became addicted to hot dogs and ragged dungarees.

Ma chose to ignore the rebuff to her compote of prunes, rationalizing to Mabel, "It's just that they're foreigners, they can't help themselves, I suppose. We have to make allowances." She wasn't about to take offense as she had it in mind to make use of their "Frenchiness" for her own ends.

In the field of cooking, Ma was an explorer, an adventurer. French cuisine, she knew, was a national treasure guarded by vows of silence. And now, right there under her thumb, were two practitioners of the secret art. Ah — ha! She waylaid them after every meal and deviously led them to expose the very foundations of their craft.

"Did you care for the trout? We always cook it in butter and cornmeal, you know — oh, you use olive oil! But just suppose you don't want to fry it ... poché ...? What's that ... oh, poached, I see. Poached in wine — well, I never! What kind of wine?"

Unaware that national secrets were being wormed out of them, Jacqueline and Madeleine talked freely, though translating French culinary terms into English was frequently beyond them. But no matter if it took a half hour of gesticulation to reveal the subtle uses of garlic, Ma persevered. From their excited chirpings she even managed to sift out a recipe for omelette aux fines herbes.

Mabel was offended by all this international atmosphere and did her best to debunk the alien contributions. Her face an angry red, she would mutter, "Whatever you call this stuff — thyme or whatever it is, looks like ants' legs — dirty. George don't care for horrid black stuff in his potato salad, I can tell you — A&P mayonnaise is what he likes, and plenty of it."

Ma paid no attention; she continued to enrich her menu with bits and pieces of Haute Cuisine long after Madeleine and Jacqueline had returned to their doting husbands.

It is impossible to imagine how Tolman Pond was described to the city-bred Belgian neighbors back home. But Ma, at least, must have been a familiar type. Ma in her steamy kitchen with her cats, her focus never leaving the pot-au-feu simmering on the back of the stove, was the epitome of that formidable personage seen in many a European café and taverna — "La Patronne."

❧ Chocolate Power

BECAUSE of her weight and arthritis, Ma was forced to use a cane. Long ago she had accepted her weight as a necessary step in her progression towards stateliness. Her massive immobility was the hub around which Tolman Pond rotated in its rackety fashion. Still, the women's page in the paper and the various magazines she read had succeeded in persuading her to be weight-conscious. She ate little. But like any good cook, while preparing a meal she tasted everything and often; she tasted up a whole meal. Of course that wasn't *eating*; she ate like a bird — but not like one of your small, insignificant birds.

Chocolate was poison, irresistible poison — she never touched it. Except just this once she'd have a bite of that delicious fudge — she wasn't *eating* it, just tasting. She had convinced herself that if she said she wasn't *eating* it, well then, of course she wasn't. Then too, if someone happened to give her a box of candy, it would be rude to refuse it.

It was a custom among Ma's regulars whenever they came back to Tolman Pond to bring her some little present or memento. This was not only evidence of their genuine feeling for her, but also good policy. When inspiration failed them over the years, they were apt to fall back on the perfect gift —

a carefully selected box of chocolates ("Wrap it, please, with a blue satin bow").

Returning to Tolman Pond after months spent out in another world where the ground was always shifting, where unease was prevalent, where nations and people were fighting and screaming at each other, the regulars counted on finding Ma in place on her kitchen stool, Wayland, brown and square, in the barn, the apple trees, Ma and Mabel in the familiar pattern. Those gifts, those boxes of candy, were tokens of their relief that in one place at least some continuity still existed. Tolman Pond was home base.

Ma accepted all gifts graciously as her due. She admired the sea-shell knick-knacks, the blue crocheted shawls, and the many handbags and knitting bags that were hung on hooks in her sitting room (useful for storing shawls and sea shells). But it was the sight of an elaborate box of chocolates that brought a gleam to her eyes.

Unfortunately, and sadly for one whose interest lay primarily in cooking, Ma had a bad stomach. Periodic rumblings shook the kitchen. Clippings of remedies, advertisements for patent medicines, panaceas that claimed to cure everything and anything were tucked into cookbooks and hidden in her baskets. Glasses filled with strange potions stood on shelves beside the sink. One week it might be onion juice, the next some weedlike substance, possibly herbs, floating in opaque water; jars and pills and bottles of powders stood in rows. None had yet proved to be the miracle cure, but there was always another to try. Her stomach was a battleground.

Under such trying conditions, a lesser character might have lost interest in preparing food. And, eyeing all those ominous pills, boarders might have entertained doubts about the cooking. Neither was the case. Ma's enthusiasm for her cuisine never wavered, nor did her guests ever lose their appetites.

With a new box of candy on her lap, Ma forgot her stomach. The ornately decorated wrapping was examined and exclaimed over. She hesitated to disturb the fancy ribbon bows, the gold and silver trimming; it seemed almost too beautiful to break into. Gloating, she'd run her fingers over the surface. Then, relishing every moment, she'd remove the paper, fold it carefully, smoothing out each crease, and tuck it into a basket. When the box was finally opened, it was so pretty she could hardly bear it — little sugar flowers, caramels wrapped in tinsel — it was a wonderland.

After this carefully orchestrated overture, Ma would study the individual chocolates intently, poking at them appraisingly like a customer at Tiffany's. Deliberately she'd select one, unwrap it with exquisite care and take a small, tentative nibble. "Oh, it has a soft center. I don't care for soft centers." With the same deliberation, she'd rewrap the reject and replace it in its tiny fluted paper cup.

Hiding the new box behind a sofa cushion, Ma would indulge herself for a few days, but eventually she would get it out and pass it around to chosen guests.

Fran and Newt always looked forward to this part of the ceremony. They watched the guests, waiting for the expression that invariably followed the discovery that every chocolate in the box, which still looked fresh from the store, had had a small bite taken out of it.

CHAPTER FOUR

◆◊ *A Fish with a Future*

FISHING, shooting, talking and skiing came as naturally to both Fran and Newt as breathing out and breathing in, and were as easy. If Ma had kept her sights trained on farming alone, this might have been a drawback, but once she changed her target to summer and weekend guests, she hit the bull's-eye. Especially after the farmhouse began to assume the proportions of a miniscule, if untidy, resort.

Having boarders in their lives had never been an affliction for either boy. They thrived on people; they liked them singly, in pairs or by the dozen. Not only had the boys been brought up in a background of diverse types, they had also been brought up by them. It was due to this grab-bag of outsiders, this marathon of personalities, that they had developed into half-native, half-summerperson hybrids, living in two worlds, at ease in both.

Unlike Ma and Wayland, who were the same with all comers at all times, Fran and Newt adjusted their mental thermostats according to the season. In the fall their vocabularies and accents took on the color of the hunter or skier, the doctor or professor; back at school, they reverted to Nelson-ese.

In winter it got dark near five. That was when the "long winter nights" began — at five. In the days before city people saw any purpose in venturing up to the wintry badlands of New Hampshire, they were isolated. If it was lonely, though, the boys didn't realize it; this was a time for reading. They drew on their supply of material, books and magazines, the backwash from migrations of summer people — a nourishing and plentiful resource.

They read and read, each selecting grist for his individual mill; they read until Wayland chunked up the furnace for the last time, until he threw out the cats at night. (The cats never minded. They instantly rounded up their friends and relatives and returned through holes in the crumbling foundations of the house, then back in by way of the tiny hatch Ma had had Wayland make in the cellar door. Strays chose whatever chair or sofa they preferred, or nested in some left-about pile of knitting — but no cat of Ma's would allow a stranger to usurp its own location. When Wayland came in at dawn, heaving in wood, banging stove lids, the strays would flee, while each of Ma's cats sat securely in its own basket.)

The cats put out, and Wayland ready to extinguish the lamps, the boys took their wrapped hot bricks or heated stone bottles of water, undressed at the head of the staircase, where it was still warm, and shot into the frigid loft, burrowing under mounds of quilts.

Now and then, to break the smothering silence of snow piling up against the windows, the boys would take an hour to indulge Ma. Newt would put his flute together and Fran would open the lid of the stained and much-abused upright Steinway and accompany Ma as she belted out hymns at the top of her capacious lungs. Ma's rendition of "From Greenland's Icy Mountains to India's Coral Strand" was a blast.

Most average evenings, the family simply read. Fran picked out novels; he was all for swashbuckling heroes, for plumes, for ringing hoofbeats. Newt ignored such trash; he went in for philosophical or controversial material. He squirreled away theories, statistics (which he adapted later to suit himself), and fusillades of contentious facts. He stored up an encyclopedic vocabulary which he practiced on his family nonstop, a habit that led his mother to hope that she was nurturing a future minister. But his bent wasn't towards the church; it was for debate.

As the winter drew on and on, the weeks longer and longer, the family's span of attention grew shorter and shorter. By April their ears were numb. And by then Newt's ideas were pent-up, restless, climbing the walls — eager for exposure and ready to stampede by the time the first guests arrived in the spring. He had a backlog of words that needed exercise, some sharp and pointed, some exotic — a vocabulary that craved air for the sheer fun of flying.

To Newt summer people were a boon, new adversaries to give his inventive brain a workout. He was loaded for action; almost any statement would start him off. He'd contradict it just to get the ball rolling. And if his opponent out of laziness or cowardice refused the challenge, Newt would change sides and chop his own postulation all to smithereens. It was stimulating, it was sport. Should the farmhouse fail to provide a worthy adversary, he'd fall back on his next favorite form of entertainment, the plausible yarn.

One evening, after a supper of Ma's special salmon mousse garnished with capers and grated hard-boiled eggs, Newt came into the living room looking for action. Nobody was there, or, if you counted old Mrs. Hill, almost nobody. Everyone else had drifted out — Fran to hunt up a game of poker, Wayland to take Mabel home, and Ma, who would come in later, was getting her kidney beans ready to soak all night. And here was Mrs. Hill, not too promising a prey.

Wayland had built a small fire on the hearth to take off

the chill, and she had settled in a rocker, which she filled nicely, and was watching the flicker of light under the black pots hanging from their cranes. She reached for her knitting. She had enjoyed the salmon but had perhaps had just one too many of those blueberry pancakes; her stomach rumbled a bit.

Newt sighed. He considered her, he considered his flute. But how dull it must be for the old girl, just sitting there; perhaps he could liven things up. He sat down beside her and, as soon as she glanced at him with a comfortable smile, he pinned her with his tense blue eyes.

"That salmon was awfully good, wasn't it? It made me realize that I've never seen a live salmon. I've read a lot about them, naturally; such a lot has been written about them. Maybe you've seen one. I know what a nature lover you are, Mrs. Hill, always observing flowers — but do you observe fish? They're interesting. The salmon gets such a lot of publicity because it's so good to eat. It's hardly fair; if other species tasted as good, we'd spend more time studying them; our brains keep a sharp eye out for our stomachs. Or perhaps it's the other way around, our stomachs keep an eye on our brains — which do you think it is, Mrs. Hill? All the salmon has an interest in is the possibility of spawning. You might say that all it thinks about is its next generation. Not that it cares about what the next generation will be up to, or its morals — no, all it cares about is producing another generation. A very limited point of view, I must say, and not very farsighted or intelligent. Right here in Tolman Pond we have fish with the same ambition, but they don't get attention like the salmon."

(Mrs. Hill's lips moved — knit one, purl two — or should it be knit one, purl one — oh dear.)

"Take that hornpout I caught last fall — are you listening, Mrs. Hill? It wasn't big even for a hornpout, but it was all I caught that day. Ma said it wasn't worth frying, and it certainly wasn't big enough to make a start for chowder, so I put it in a bowl on the kitchen table until I could get more. But what with one thing and another I didn't get around to fishing again. So there it was. At meals we'd feed him crumbs and stuff, and he'd swim about getting plump and happy — he was company, too. We named him Alfred. When we called, he'd come to the surface for food, even jump for it. It seemed to me that he was rather precocious; his whiskers had a clever look. Now, having him right there to observe every day, I decided to compile a case history of the Native Hornpout, compare his intelligence with the overrated salmon's. So I kept a notebook and jotted down the time when he first jumped into my hand for food. I began to consider training him to do somersaults like a dolphin; it would be a first for the small-fish world. Then he got so that he didn't want to return to his bowl, and finally I made him a platform so that he could jump out whenever he was in the mood. He was so contented there that we just took the bowl away altogether — oh, we had to give him water, we sprinkled him regularly. Ma kept an eye out, and she'd say, 'Newt, go out and fetch me some pieces of good dry maple and sprinkle Alfred on the way.' She had one of those bottles with a perforated top they used for ironing. It was handy, and Ma never let anyone walk by without giving Alfred his sprinkle. So he stayed fat, damp and comfortable like a member of the family. A fish with a real bright future. My case history seemed sure to make a contribution to piscatorial science, wouldn't you say? I'm afraid you've dropped a stitch, Mrs. Hill — can I help? — but what harm can one more hole do? Knitting seems to be nothing but holes loosely held together by strings of wool anyway. But now — about Alfred. One day Mabel put a vase of flowers on the table, and when they'd faded, she took them out — but she left one petal floating, and Alfred, who had gotten a little above himself, mistook it for a landing platform, jumped, missed and drowned."

❧ The Perfect Hunting Dog

THE WOODS, the diminishing fields, were as familiar to Fran and Newt as the beaten track between the attic where they slept and the kitchen, barn and henhouse. On their way to school they had taken shortcuts, and when they drove the cows to an upland pasture, they followed old logging roads and woods trails. Many were the grassy roads that Fran showed me when we rode together.

As soon as he was old enough to have a gun, Fran had stalked these woods on foot. He didn't walk, he stalked. Natives, as a rule, despised walking for the sake of walking; that was for summer people and included perpetual talking. Stalking was different — no conversation and more listening. In the spring Fran and Newt stalked fish in streams and ponds; in the summer they stalked girls — well, any season.

It was after the boarders left in the autumn that Fran stalked the woods, the canny native padding through the brush Indian fashion, trying for a single flash shot at some wily partridge. If he ever brought one down, it was a triumph of marksmanship and luck. To Ma, the time he put in wasn't justified by the amount of meat he supplied to the family fare; she tolerated it on the basis that it was just one of those innate urges of the average male that had to be put up with, and now and then paid off.

Killing wasn't the goal for Fran; stalking meant more than that. It meant standing away from humans for an hour or two; it meant breathing in stillness; it meant absorption of the forest scent and simply watching one brown leaf lazily drift down to settle beside another brown leaf. But he would never have been there at all if it weren't that he was stalking something, searching for something, in pursuit — in silence.

Ordinarily silence had few charms for Fran. For the most part he enjoyed people for companionship. He liked games, all games, and he needed partners. He corralled guests for poker, for tennis, for riding picnics. He took them fishing, and sometimes they crept along behind him when he hunted. ("Hunting" to me still means banging away with a gun at any old thing. I know I should differentiate. "Hunting" is banging away at an animal; "shooting" means banging away at a bird; but I use either word interchangeably.)

Come November every man in Nelson set out to get his deer, and city sports poured in to get theirs. There were few outsiders before that deadly season. City folk didn't appreciate creeping through brambles and swamps, tearing holes in expensive pants, in the faint hope of getting a shot at a bird that was invariably either out of sight or out of range. But then bird dogs were introduced and the whole picture changed.

There had always been rabbit dogs, coon dogs, and a few foxhounds around. But none of the locals had a setter or a pointer and even if they had ever heard of such a thing, it would have been an extravagance beyond considering. Bird dogs had been used exclusively in the South. Fran's first bird dog was sent up to him by a friend who shot quail in Virginia, a dog that had proved too slow to be good in open land. "Tippy" was a setter, a carelessly designed setter; he drooled, and his pants hung down in back. He was slow all right, deliberately, insultingly slow, which Fran claimed a virtue as he wouldn't always be "bumping" birds. Having this paragon of dogs transformed Fran from an idle, happy-go-lucky, spontaneous hunter into a professional guide. He still did just what he had been doing, but now got paid for it into the bargain. He acquired a Guide's License, very official, and a shiny badge with the State insignia. Now he had the opportunity to go all out in the role of a "native guide," become laconic and quaint. He remained his usual, loquacious self and shared his enthusiasm for hunting with kindred souls. It was no sacrifice to give up his lonely stalking. He let Tippy play that part, and after a shot, Fran hooted, hollered and shouted directions for locating the possibly downed bird.

Tippy had both style and talent. Fran willingly endured Tippy's style because of his talent. That talent lay in his infallible nose, an indispensable asset in following a running or walking bird. Tippy took his time, he wouldn't be hurried, but like any renowned tracker he was sure to get his man. He didn't cheat (not in the field, anyway); when he pointed to a bird, he wasn't fooling — it was there.

His style was something else again. He could, if he was in the mood, hold the traditional stance, the classic point — tail up, one foot raised, neck stretched ahead — but if he thought Fran was too long in getting to him, he'd lie down, take a snooze. Good bird dog that he was, asleep or not, his nose was on the job, pointing dead on to the hidden bird.

Tippy was not lovable. He and Fran had a workable relationship based on common interests, but Tippy and I barely tolerated one another. Horses he liked; he was attracted by their smell. He would follow any horse. So, more often than not, when I went riding, he would skulk along behind, keeping out of range until it was too late for me to send him home. It didn't matter to me whether he was along or not, except that he was a thief. Whenever we went by a house, Tippy would sneak around to the back and snatch whatever was lying loose. Once as I was riding through the outskirts of Dublin, he dashed out from behind a plushy house with a whole leg of lamb in his jaws. Since I was too cowardly to get into a hassle, I kicked my horse into a canter and fled. Tippy paced along behind with his loot.

After one of these expeditions he didn't come back. Fran was worried (I couldn't have cared less). He called neighbors and put up Lost Dog notices in the grocery store and the post office — still no Tippy. I began to have hope. Finally word came through the grapevine that Perley Swett had a dog in his woodshed and he wished someone would take it away. Of course it was Tippy, and of course Perley wanted to get rid of him.

Backtracking, we figured that on the day that Tippy disappeared, Tippy and I had crossed paths with a group of campers out for a ride. Several horses would have smelled more than a single, so Tippy changed horses in midstream and tagged after them until in turn they had crossed paths with old Mrs. Swett, driving her horse and buggy back from Keene, and he transferred again.

Since I was due to make a shopping trip, it was up to me to pick him up on my way home.

The Swetts lived at the remote end of nowhere. At one time, many years before, that road had connected two small towns, but all the residents that lived along it except the Swetts had moved away, and the road had been "thrown up." In the best of times it hadn't been much; now it was just two ruts wandering through the woods, mulching its way past cellar holes, past the crumbling remains of a sheep barn, around boulders, down ledges. A road made by wagon wheels and suitable only for wagon wheels.

As the car inched across a dry brookbed, ahead I could see the woods opening into a sunny glade of brilliant green grass and jonquils. A large flock of goats scrambled out from a barn and surrounded the car.

The Swetts' house was weathered grey, the clapboards curled and brittle, the grooves in the front door deeply channeled. Supporting the house on one side was a shed containing a tangle of old boards, old wheels, old machinery, and a white bathtub to water the goats.

Perley himself was dapper in overalls, a red handkerchief round his neck, and his white hair aflourish on the sides of his brown, bald skull. He pushed his way through the goats.

He was real glad, he said, that someone had come for that dog. He'd tied it up behind, couldn't stand it in the house. That dog, he said, ate up all the goats' food and made them fidgety; besides, they didn't take to his stink.

Perley explained that he'd been slow to get the word out because his mother had been poorly and he didn't like to leave her. In fact, she'd been in bed for days, just lay there — hadn't seen anybody — she just *lay* there — he wondered whether it might do her good to see someone, might stir her up some. Maybe I would stop in a minute?

She was in one of the two front rooms; it had probably been the parlor. (The other must have been the kitchen, but the glimpse I got revealed nothing but tables piled up with cans, newspapers, bottles, and more and more papers.) Mrs. Swett was lying on a bed so low it seemed only a foot off the floor. Later I realized that this must have been because there were no bedsprings; the mattress was laid across ropes strung on the frame. An old hound dog dozed at the foot and raised his head briefly as I entered. A table beside the bed held an assortment of patent medicines and a jelly glass with wilted daisies. The rest of the room was crowded with bulging burlap sacks. What could they have held? Perley was obviously afflicted with pack-rat-itis.

It may have been her features or perhaps her expression that made her seem so beautiful — whatever it was, she had a kind of beauty as natural as a shaft of light. Her face was delicate, fine-boned, her skin hazel brown, her hair fresh and white. Something about her made me think of an idealized portrait of an American Indian, her eyes were so dark, so self-contained and peaceful. It was the face of one who was waiting, without fear.

Stirring her up was the last thing I wanted to do. We talked quietly about the peaches that I had just bought in Keene. The one she held in her thin, brown hand looked gross and fleshy in comparison.

On the way home with Tippy, whose natural malodor was now fortified with goat, we bumped back through the same dry brookbed. But now my point of view had sharpened; it seemed to me that it wasn't completely dry after all. Among the rocks was a tiny clear stream, a mini-brook, a mere thread that bypassed pebbles and trickled along under dams of twigs and leaves. Small and bright, it serenely followed a course laid out for it by some natural law.

Back home, after I returned Tippy to Fran's welcoming arms, the car had to be swept, scrubbed and deodorized. But I didn't begrudge the effort. If it hadn't been for Tippy, I wouldn't have had that glimpse of Mrs. Swett before she died. Tippy's one good deed.

⁓ℰ Bushwhackers

MA AND HUNTERS were made for one another; the relationship was warm and boisterous. As she had never paid any attention to the condition of the farmhouse to begin with, the fact that now it was more of a shambles than ever didn't bother her at all. Dogs and assorted gear covered the floor space, tables were smeared with gun oil, damp clothing trailed down the staircase and hung over the backs of chairs. She encouraged the hunters to put their muddy boots under the stove; their odor mingled with the flavors from the stew pot.

The one area where she and they might very well have locked horns was the matter of alcohol. Ma hated drinking and had a horror that her two innocent boys might be corrupted. This danger zone was recognized by both sides and avoided by an unspoken pact. The hunters kept their bottles out of sight, and Ma turned a blind eye when, after the table had been set, water glasses vanished into bedrooms. Later, she was willing to accept their praise of her cooking no matter how polluted with whiskey it might be.

For a number of years Fran was the sole guide in the county; he had territorial rights. But this was too good to last, and eventually his area was invaded and the sport took on a new dimension. To outwit rival guides, he had to be perpetually on the lookout for new, unexplored hunting grounds, for the Shangri-La where birds would be waiting in fearless innocence. He knew, of course, there was no such place. The best he could do was to try to hide all traces of each foray from rival troops. Specific locations had code names, like "White Horse Cover" or "Witch's Cover." The enemy had their own set of code names for the same spots, to them, "Bedspring" and "Wellhouse." Both sides were crestfallen when they found telltale shotgun shells in their secret grounds.

Sometimes I met Fran and his followers at a prearranged place, say the double-arched stone bridge in Stoddard. Not as a hunter — far from it — I was gun-shy. At the first blast my impulse was to drop flat and start burrowing. My role was lunch-basket carrier, though now and then I tagged along behind, well out of range, curious to see what it was all about. To my dismay, I found it easy to catch the fever, to be infected by the excitement of the chase.

Fran had a routine program of procedure. Finished eating, the doctors or businessmen or whatever they might be would watch their guru for his signal that lunch break was over. When it came, they instantly changed character, becoming tribesmen steeling themselves to face jungle dangers. In silence, each would check his gun, load it carefully (many of those guns were prized family possessions as cherished as a Rolls Royce) and wait for Fran, the Headman, to assign them positions. As soon as he moved off, they entered the brush stealthily, senses alert for the sound of the dog's bell. When the bell stopped and Fran gave a low, significant whistle, it was a sign that the dog was on a point (or asleep), and the hunters would move in for the kill. At this juncture, I always held my breath, crossed the fingers of my right hand to prevent the hunter from missing his shot, and crossed the fingers of my left hand to prevent the bird from being killed.

By now I had almost become resigned to the bloody feathers, had almost accepted the fact that small creatures of the woods were rarely allowed to die a peaceable death. When a bird grew heavy with age, a weasel would slide up and choke its life out, or a fox would tear it to pieces. There is no retirement home for decrepit birds — they are destined to be recycled, but not in comfort. One can't blame the fox, he is due his meal . . . but why can't he be satisfied with a mouse?

No, not a mouse, I'm on the side of the mouse — it has such exquisite ears and tiny feet. After all, millions of years have gone into the development of that miniature mechanism, into perfecting those internal tubes and springs, those organs fit for digesting bugs, those threads of muscle. What a ridiculous waste it is that all those working parts, so carefully fitted together in an economical space, end up as fuel for another, larger mechanism.

So there I would be, flat on the ground, the picnic basket upside down, my face scrunched in bristly leaves, straining to hear the shots that would tell me which hand had won this time.

At dusk they all came back to the farm, groaning, with sore muscles, broken eyeglasses, lacerated skin, but elated whether they had bagged any game or not.

This elation didn't derive from simply blowing a couple of birds to bits, but rather from the pursuit itself, the chase. The urge to pursue is innate, whether hiding under a conservative business suit, disguised as a need to bring off a big deal, or masquerading as an altruistic search for a lost work of art. It is the pursuit itself, of a hope, a dream, a deal that keeps the world on its toes.

It was pursuit that had brought these hunters to the rocky highlands, to track the wily, wary bird, to make the perfect shot. This was their spoken goal. Underneath was the urge to cast off the pin-striped suit, to cut loose from the office, to get back to square one. It was a chance to test whether senses had become blunted by stringent pressures of business, to test whether eyes, ears and hands still had the ability to coordinate in split-second timing, to give feet accustomed to prepared turf or pavement an opportunity to re-experience earth in its original state.

For the hunters, today had provided a refresher course in listening to the delicate sounds of the woods, the sudden whirs, the mysterious rustles, the silence. They felt they had passed — gave themselves, say, a B-, not bad, not bad at all.

Exhausted, satisfied, they sat in collapsed ease by the fire, glasses discreetly out of sight, and rehashed every minute of the day: the shots that missed (the bird flew the wrong way); the dog that mortified his owner by chasing a rabbit (he had a cold, was too fat, or too thin, the scent was weak); the gun that misfired (that's what comes of lending your gun for duck-shooting; believe me I won't do that again in a hurry).

If it had been Tippy who had been the working dog that day — Tippy, Fran's pride and joy — he would have distinguished himself, been the perfect little gentleman, retrieving lost birds in his masterly, slovenly fashion, and now he would be lying there on the rug in comfort, slobbering with self-satisfaction.

If they had been lucky the previous day and able to present Ma with a couple of birds, they could look forward to game roasted to perfection, stuffed and glossy with butter. They might even receive her gracious permission to open a bottle of wine.

Starting out with nothing but chill promise and green hope, the day had left them drained, yet round and replete, glowing in the firelight like plum puddings topped off with flickers of brandy.

◄ Green Tomato Pickles

TIPPY DIDN'T last forever, not quite. After him, Fran got two young setters with pedigrees, untrained, giddy and over-enthusiastic. He worked with them daily, trying to wear them down before the season opened.

I went with him one day when he wanted to look over some territory on the far side of town as possible bird cover. So with the dogs in the back of the station wagon, we took the hilly road from the village. Besides being as eager as the dogs to see what I could see, hear what I could hear, and smell what I could smell, I always had the hope in the back of my mind that local people I met when I was with Fran might accept me as his wife, might forgive my background.

The air was effervescent, lemon-sharp; the wooded hills

flamboyant with sumac. Weeds and small pines crowded the fields on either side. The porch of the first house we came to was overflowing with collateral (Fran's word) — a washing machine, sap buckets, a broken wheelbarrow. There was a person up on the back roof who dodged out of sight as we passed, arousing my curiosity. Fran would know who it was.

"Oh sure, it's Maggy Herschel. I went to school with her." I wanted to slow down a little to see what she was doing, but Fran kept right on. "No, we won't stop now; she's shingling the roof. As a matter of fact, we really haven't seen her at all." I looked blank. Fran explained. "You see, she always lets on it's Willy does those things like shingling, or cleaning out the well. She'd be put out if we stopped by now, with Willy sitting in the parlor probably reading a comic." He drove on by. "Willy is really fond of Maggy, he really is. He doesn't aim to be watching if a rung on that old ladder breaks."

"You're making it up!"

"No, I'm not. I went to school with Willy too, don't forget." He went on, talking to himself: "There just might be some bird cover behind the Tuttle house, I suppose, looks like a few wild grapes." This house was crumbling, almost hidden under jungle growth. Some old apple trees were snarled together, half bent to the ground; among them a small stump moved.

"Hey — I saw something moving back there!"

"That's probably old Granny Tuttle herself," Fran said. "I bet she's pushing ninety — wonder if she'll last the winter."

"What's she doing — stop just one minute!"

But Fran kept going, and the bent figure didn't turn towards the road.

"She's looking for something — see, she's poking about with a stick, nuts maybe, or an old apple or two, something she can make use of." I craned my neck, bothered; I had an urge to do something, to help somehow or other, but Fran was firm. "No, leave her alone. If she stopped now, it might make her lose her place out there among the leaves. She'd be upset, it'd put her out for the rest of the day." We had passed the place by now.

"But suppose she was starving, how would you like that!"

He was unperturbed. "She may be, I suppose. She just may starve this winter. It'll never be on her mind, though. It won't fret her the way it would you. You see, her mind is all taken up with small, exciting problems like finding apples with no worm holes. And if she does find a good, solid one, it'll make her whole day, I promise you." Unconvinced, I persisted.

"But she seems so alone — maybe not enough to eat, it seems sad . . . Back in New Jersey people like her are taken care of; she'd be in a home, three good meals a day and all."

"Yeah, I know. But she'd die just the same, of boredom probably. Here, she's really living while she's dying. She'll be so intent on those small excitements, she won't even notice when it comes. Don't worry so — honestly, we do keep an eye on her. Martin gave her a few old hens last week; I bet they're in her kitchen right now for company. And suppose, just suppose one of those hens should lay an egg! It'd give Granny a bigger charge than you ever got from a double martini." To reassure me further, he added that he'd come by one evening and chop up some of those old apple branches and leave them where they'd be handy.

"Now, here's the place I've been looking for, the Baileys'. They've gone for the winter, and there's an alder run at the top of that field I always thought looked promising."

"And who are the Baileys?"

"The Baileys are natives, an old family. But they don't stay here in the winter any more. The two sisters teach somewhere in Massachusetts, and the brother, Horace — he's a mite odd."

He went to the back of the car and let loose the dogs, who could hardly wait for the tailgate to be let down before lunging out. They surged around excitedly, then jumped over the wall to explore the field. "Just look at those damn fools, how am I ever going to get them in shape — crazy as chickens." He watched them in disgust and turned to me. "D'you want to come up the hill with me? It'll be pretty." I decided against it; he'd be longer than he thought, he always was.

"I'll stay here — look for some small excitement."

Whistling to the dogs, Fran followed them over the wall, calling back, "Try to find an apple without a worm hole."

The car was parked under a row of big maples through which the sun poured like hot buttered rum. The house looked closed. Well, more half closed — some windows were boarded up and some not. The grass had been recently cut, no weeds. There were a lot of funny little white things — golf balls? Mothballs? No, of course not, they were mushrooms, those little puffballs that are good to eat, come up right after a rain and then go by quickly, turning brown and squashy. It seemed a shame to let them go to waste. I picked a few; they were firm and fresh.

Making a sack out of the front of my sweater, I began to pick in earnest. I picked on both sides of the house and ended up back in front. I could hear Fran a long way off, hollering at his dogs; he'd be quite a while still.

The long, narrow front porch shaded the whole width of the house. One window was unboarded; would it be antiquey inside, or Sears Roebucky? No harm in taking a peek. But even on the porch I couldn't see inside; I kept getting my own reflection. So I went right up close and put my nose to the glass. *There was a face!* — a face pressed to mine from the inside! I jumped back, feeling as if I'd had an electric shock. Both frightened and dismayed, caught snooping and scavenging on private property — I wanted to run.

But it was too late. With a squall of rusty hinges, the door was forced open and a loud, rough voice shouted, "HAVE YOU GOT A RECIPE FOR GREEN TOMATO PICKLES?"

My mind tripped over its feet and fell flat. Before I could begin to think at all, Horace — it had to be Horace — turned away, muttering, "You'll need something to put those mushrooms in." He groped around inside the house, then thrust out a battered candy box, his voice, now that it was broken in, more in control of its decibels. "Here, this'll do, I guess. But you see, I've got all these tomatoes, must be at least three bushels, all green" — he sounded distraught — "the frost'll get them. I've got to do *something*." He was closing the door without waiting for an answer. As if I had any. But then the door reopened a crack and his harsh voice blew through in a plaintive gust, "I don't care for pickles. I don't care for them at *all*."

The door closed. The house again looked blank, vacant.

Fran was coming down the field, his dogs at heel, their tongues hanging down to their knees. "Found some signs of woodcock up there. Thought those idiot dogs were going to take off on a rabbit track, but I caught them in time. How about you? Did you find any small — oh, mushrooms, great! Free groceries. Hope you weren't too bored just hanging around?"

No, I hadn't been bored. And I had made a small, invisible breakthrough, a secret triumph — a native had asked me for a recipe — a crack had appeared in that fence.

Ma sautéed the mushrooms with a little onion, cream and sherry. We had them on toasted slabs of homemade bread with crisp bacon on the side.

CHAPTER FIVE

∽ Let It Snow, Let It Snow, Let It Snow

SKIERS followed on the heels of the bird shooters; often they were the same heels. Hunters who came up for the last of the shooting season sometimes found that they were snowed in. Fran and Newt instantly turned to skiing. They skied in the pasture or on one of the shortcuts to school or on an abandoned logging road. On the ensuing weekends, the bird shooters left their guns at home and brought skis.

Fran never became a first-rate skier and didn't care. He had a foursquare crouch that got him down slopes right side up. It was Newt who was the star, the real skier; he had flair, he was sensational. Also resourceful and inventive — if his skis didn't suit the type of snow for that day, he tinkered them up. He made one pair of stepped skis, guaranteed to get him up any hill without sliding, and he schussed down on his own miniature staircase. If the snow on the pasture hill was too soft, too icy, or nonexistent, he made use of the pond. Skiers were towed on the ice behind skidding cars, and if that surface proved to be monotonously flat, Newt built obstacles which could be jumped over or crashed into.

Neither Fran nor Newt had a sport outfit; anything went. Fran fancied a pair of white flannel tennis slacks, Edwardian in cut, bought at a Ladies Aid sale. Newt was resplendent in dress trousers with a satin stripe down the side, though after a winter spent abroad his style changed. He blossomed into an Austrian loden-cloth jacket with bone buttons and became a Pro. He gave lessons, wrote articles, and had his picture taken doing stunts.

By hook and by crook a rope-driven ski tow was built, and every hook and crook had to be maintained by the mechanical genius of a local man who had spent a lifetime coping with cranky machinery. The tow's motor never took to servicing skiers; anything was an excuse for it to die. One skier too many and it disgorged clouds of smoke, hiccuped, and quit.

The rope itself was a hand-me-down from the Cheshire Mills, which had recently converted to electricity. Worn and frayed, the rope either broke or froze or twisted and had to be frequently spliced. No one could ever be sure which piece of equipment would work or not work.

And yet skiers came — and came — and came. For the local people, the tow was a nine-days' wonder; they came to gawk, nudging one another, snickering at the antics going on. This was, of course, before the ski business burgeoned and busted out all over New England like one of those zucchini plants that take over the whole garden.

The farmhouse was overrun. You'd think Ma would have been suffocated, swamped, but nothing of the sort. She took it in her stride, driving Mabel and Wayland to heights of accomplishment hitherto undreamed of (and undesired). Fran and Newt were in their element; they loved it all. Fran was able to exercise his natural inclination to be the genial host, the all-purpose master of ceremonies. He was the raconteur; he was there to unload bags, build fires, filch glasses from under Ma's nose; he would even wash dishes (or get the guests to do it) and make beds. It suited his gregarious nature to have people all around him.

The earliest contingent of skiers consisted of Sam Mason's old habitués. Broken in by Sam, they accepted Ma as a replacement, and the farmhouse was their refuge from affluent comfort. They already knew how to get there, but for newcomers, finding the way wasn't easy. Tolman Pond wasn't on the map, and to locate Nelson took a magnifying glass. Directions proved to be a nightmare, often misleading them into a hostile wasteland where survival seemed dubious. Finally, in desperation, the newcomer would stop at that sorry-looking farmhouse to ask the way. He had already passed it twice without giving it a thought, as it was obviously not the place he was looking for, not at all the type that Charley Norton would have recommended. The best he could hope for was that he wouldn't be met by some deaf, blithering old fool and his snarling dogs.

What a relief it was to have the door opened by Fran, looking every inch the country host, and to see behind him the familiar members of the St. Botolph Club. In no time at all, the traveler would be settled by the fire, and in less time than that was getting an answer to the all-important question, "Say — how do you go about getting ice in this place? Off the roof! Well, OK, I'll get it . . ." By the time Fran brought him into the kitchen to meet Ma and Mabel, his state of mind would have radically improved.

On her stool by the kitchen table, Ma worked over a big, flat casserole, covering it with crumbs. She wiped her hands on her apron to take his hand and greet him.

"So, you're that friend of Charley's — how is he? The last time he was here, he had the quinsy sore throat. I advised him — Mabel, just hand down that bottle of herb vinegar from the top shelf — can't reach it! Of course you can, Mabel, use a chair — well, now, that's good of you, Mr. Er-m-m (not quite his name but near enough), it's useful being so tall. Well, as I was saying, I advised Charley to take a good dose of lemon and honey. We were all out of honey, but maple syrup did just as well — he took it, but you know, I suspect he added something to it . . . he got well just a little *too* fast. He'd have to pay for it in the long run, and that's what I told him, but you know Charley, there are times when he's real pigheaded. WAYLAND! — is that the henhouse door banging again? If the latch doesn't work, for heaven's sake why don't you drive a spike in, I can't abide a door that bangs. Mabel, how much vinegar are you using? Be careful. We're having scalloped oysters tonight; Charley is partial to my scalloped oysters, and as you're his friend, you might be too. Fran, will you set that kettle back further? Do I smell something burning? — Oh, Mr. Er-m-m, I'm afraid you leaned against the stove! Mabel! Rub a little of the vinegar into the spot. It'll lift the smell and since it's brown vinegar, you'll never notice the hole . . ." By the time the newcomer returned to the living room, he had been well broken in.

The farm didn't cater to the needs of the guests; the shoe was apt to be on the other foot. Beds were in every-old-where; people had to scramble for the use of inadequate bathrooms. If it was psychological roughage these guests craved, they surely got it.

Ma was a believer in the no-coddling principle. That went for the boarders and livestock both. The nearby presence of animals was very evident from their bawling, their cackling and their smells. Wayland reported what they were eating, Ma knew their daily input and output; she made shocking inquiries into their private functions. They were to be properly fed and cared for — but not coddled. The same went for the boarders; she watched over their welfare and knew all their deplorable habits.

Mabel was the stool pigeon; she spied the bottles concealed under beds, she tattled on cans of sardines that were passed, dripping, across bed pillows. At meals, she was stationed at the pass-through in the wall between the dining room and kitchen, and offenders who didn't clean up their plates would find that they received half-portions at the next meal. If they then went humbly to ask for seconds, Ma would grant this graciously like any good housemother.

The kitchen was choked with skiers. Ma enjoyed this; she kept an eye on each and exacted her toll of compliments as each stopped for a word in passing. But if, while idly chatting, someone reached for a sample of whatever was being prepared, he'd get his hand slapped. Each spoonful had been counted — there were no extras. "Don't touch that bacon! That piece is for Duckett, he hasn't had his yet —" It was turmoil. But over the clatter Ma's voice would rise loud in song, expressing an unlikely wish: "ROCK of AGES, cleft for ME — Mabel, you're not chopping those onions fine enough — let me HIDE myself in THEE — ."

❧ They Speak Only to God

INGENIOUS as they are, New Englanders aren't much at producing reliable weather. There'll be those splendid days, vivid blue-and-white flag-waving days, perfect wash-day Mondays, days that stir the blood and raise hopes, and then — thump, the shade is pulled down.

In January snow is a reasonably safe bet, blankets of fluffy snow toppling off branches, perfect for making long winding tracks down a hillside. One January in particular, snow had been predicted, so of course there was none. Not just a teasingly inadequate amount — none at all.

One family with children hadn't canceled. Since the weather in town was equally unsatisfactory, they chose to let the Tolmans bear the brunt of a possibly disappointing vacation rather than cope with their children in town. And there was also Duckett Jones, a doctor who came when he felt like it, regardless of weather.

They stood in the barn doorway staring out at the dry, brown grass, at the soggy-iced pond no good for skating. Fran expressed the general feeling, "Look at that — there isn't a piece of snow big enough to blow your nose on." They considered this statement and agreed.

There was nothing for it; they'd have to have a picnic somewhere, somehow.

Turning to Wayland, Fran said, "What would you think of the Cabot place, Pop? That'd be good for a picnic today, don't you think? We could have some trapshooting."

"Won't the Cabots mind?" Duckett asked.

"Nope," said Wayland, "they won't mind."

Ma was alerted and transferred the chowder into a pail; then she and Mabel went to work on a big batch of biscuits.

Everyone was to hike up except Wayland, who loaded the lunch, the guns, the clay pigeons and the boomerang gimmick that hurled the clay frisbees into the air into the pickup truck. When the biscuits were ready, he took the long way around and met the rest at the top of the hill.

The trail was pale, crunchy, like shredded wheat. The beeches held their amber leaves, and the generally muted colors of the landscape were intermittently broken by raucous streaks of blue-jay blue. Busybody chickadees tagged along, hopping from twig to twig. The two farm goats had been allowed to come for a winter treat; they loved a picnic. They'd lag behind, browsing, and then suddenly make a mad dash to catch up, bowling over any stragglers or children in their path.

After an hour's climb the group trudged by a vacant, narrow brick house with broken windows, on by a huge sheep barn with a slumped-in roof, and up to the high field. Here Wayland had already started a fire and put the pail of chowder on to heat.

The view was panoramic — Monadnock front stage as usual. The spire of the Harrisville church rose like a white chalk slash against the heavy green and brown of the woods that stretched endlessly on all sides. A creek glimmered down in the hollow, a thread connecting two lakes. Everything except the pink brick house and barn immediately below was smothered in trees.

Fran collected the family and their three boys and went farther up to arrange the shoot, the goats tearing along out of curiosity. "Call us when the soup's hot!"

Duckett settled down beside Wayland, pulling a flask out of a hip pocket and offering it to him.

"Now, Wayland," he said, "what's all this about Cabots anyway? You're not claiming that *that* is a real Cabot house — not the *Boston* Cabots?"

"Well, sure — Boston Cabots or some such, don't know which ones, they come and go, we don't know one from another . . . some don't speak English, you know.

"Last summer," he continued, "damned if their cow didn't come down to my garden again. I didn't aim to pay it much mind — what's a cabbage or two anyway — but Sadie got wind of it and nothing would do but I had to leave my coffee and come all the way up here. I banged on the door, and this Cabot came out — well, he wasn't all that much of a Cabot, more of a Lithuanian — a woodchopper — all smiles and brown teeth. I was some riled on account of the hike, and I said, 'Your damn cow is down in my garden again!' And he looks happy as hell and says, 'Yah, yah, he *like* garden.' So I made out good and plain what he could do with his cow and my garden. He was real hurt-like. 'You no like cow? Well, OK,

OK,' and he goes into the house and comes out with this brown paper bag. 'Now,' he says, 'I get cow.' So we both take off through the woods to the garden and there is his cow, chomping away. So this Cabot opens his paper bag and takes out a sandwich. He scrunches down, holding it out to the cow, and creeps up, calling in a wheedly voice, 'Nice cow, nice cow — here's some yummy, yummy, yummy!' And as soon as the cow put her head out towards the sandwich, he lets out this yell and belts the cow in the face. The bread-and-lard sandwich busts all to pieces, and the cow gallops off with Cabot right behind. That's the last I've seen of him, and I'm glad of it."

Duckett considered this, turning it round and round in his mind. "But all the same, Wayland, he wasn't what you'd call a real Cabot, was he?"

"Sure he was — lived here, didn't he? So he was a Cabot, has to be. I suppose there's all sorts of Cabots — no end to 'em, I'd say. We get all kinds; what kind do you have in Boston?"

The chowder was hot by now and improved by a great dollop of brandy that Duckett sloshed in. The goats cavorted about, happy in their job as a portable disposal unit. One distinguished himself by leaping first into the body of the truck and from there to the top of the cab, where he posed, goatee blowing in the breeze, like Balboa surveying the Pacific. (He may have had a drop of brandy.) When the chowder and biscuits were finished off, everyone had another bout of shooting, and then the boys, having had all the fresh air they could stand and satisfied that they had triumphed over the unwanted peace and quiet of the day, decided to go back in the truck with Wayland, the goats and the leftovers.

The parents, with Fran and Duckett, were in no hurry and made themselves comfortable on the grass to give their digestions time to cope. Before them Monadnock stood in quiet grandeur, the Green Mountains were a wispy outline in the west, and Boston was an unseen rumor in the east.

"There must have been hundreds of sheep in sight from up here," Fran speculated, "all these hills were open, rocky, of course, but open. When the wool market went to hell, the open land went too. And now look what's left — pines and scrub. Soon the scrub will smother the blueberries, and the pines will shove right up through the rotten roof of the barn — and it'll go."

"The house doesn't look too good either," said Duckett. "Why don't the Cabots keep it up — not that I believe that there was ever a Cabot here."

"Oh, yes there was! There was a Cabot, and I can prove it — it may have been a little before my time, but you see I have a photographic memory for things I've never seen. Back, say, about nineteen hundred, there was this Cabot on the lookout for a suitable hobby. All his friends had hobbies. For the most part they collected things — paintings, or shoe buttons or yachts — they'd copped the market in all those fields. But this Cabot finally latched on to something new — he collected farms. At first he bought one or two modest little ones, thinking to fix them up as showpieces. But he got carried away, kept hearing about these rare one-of-a-kind farms, and before he knew it, he was up to his neck in farms, but even then he couldn't stop; he was hooked.

"He came through southern New Hampshire like a scourge, buying abandoned farms right and left. He drove right up here in his gleaming, brass-bound Packard. His chauffeur, an old hand at reading the boss's mind, stopped for Mr. Cabot to get out. The farmer, or sheeptender, came to the door with his whole family crowding behind him, bug-eyed with excitement. Mr. Cabot approached in dignity, in his imported English tweeds, with his gold-headed cane and his straw hat on just so. He tipped his hat courteously, and the farmer, not to be outdone, took his off and flattened it to the bosom of his overalls. Mr. Cabot continued towards the front of the house, taking care to avoid chicken droppings, and said, 'Good morning, what an extremely pleasant place you have here, and such a pleasing view! Now, I do wonder whether by any chance it might be for sale?'

"The farmer, mournful as a walrus, scratched himself thoughtfully and looked for a place where he could spit without offense, then said in a voice cracking with gloom, 'No, it ain't. I'd sell it — sell it like a shot. But I hafter say that a year or so before I settled in here, I heard tell that it had been bought by an old fool from Boston named Louis Cabot. Now, you wouldn't be needing a hound pup, would you? I got some real good ones back in the kitchen . . . ' "

❧ That Fat Pink Cloud? That's Lily

WHEN DUCKETT Jones came, he was usually loaded up to his chin with brown paper bags that clinked. Coming into the kitchen, he would first give Ma a big kiss and, without putting anything down, steal a hot roll and begin to rummage about in his collection of cocktail tidbits for his present for her. *If* he managed this without any of his bags splitting open, he would step over a cat or two and plunge into the living room to see who was there and offer them a drink. If it should happen that it was someone who had come up for a quiet weekend in the country, he could forget it. With Duckett, there was no such thing.

Sometimes he came alone, but more often he brought a group of other doctors with him. They all, on leaving their respective hospitals, shucked off every vestige of sterilized formality. It was as if they craved release from their sanitary, clinical atmosphere and found it in Ma's kitchen. Some of them had been coming regularly to shoot with Fran, but most, like Duckett, were skiers. One might assume that knowing what they did of the fragility of the human body, they would respect their own bones. Nothing of the sort! They slammed down hills with abandon, hooting like maniacs. When one struck a tree and had a possible fracture, they fixed him up with a makeshift splint and, leaving him beside the fire in Ma's care and borrowing an axe, went out to chop down the tree.

Duckett, with his wilted shirt, bald, freckled head, brown sparkly eyes and infectious grin, was irresistible, and looked anything but a portentous medical man. A favorite of Ma's despite those clinking bottles, he very nearly lost his place in her affections over *l'affaire Lily*.

He had phoned from Boston in the middle of the week, saying that there was a good pig in his lab that had been used for blood samples. The experiment was completed and here was a pig — a squeaky-clean pig, free for the taking. A free pig! Ma's eyes lit up; visions of pig's knuckles danced in her head. Unhesitatingly she backed Duckett's suggestion that Fran and I come to Town, have a festive evening, spend the night, and next day drive back home with the loot.

A junket like that was a rare treat. We spent hours washing, curling, pressing and starching ourselves and set off in Wayland's old Chevy sedan with burlap sacks piled on the back seat.

The first stage of our trip included a visit to Duckett's lab, where he introduced us to his two friendly chimpanzees. They were a little too friendly for my taste, as they kept running their dry, bony hands up and down my legs and peeking under my skirt. But they were as dear to Duckett as his family, and indeed there was a resemblance. He had a photo of the three of them, faces pressed together. Duckett's was the one with the happy smile — the other two looked very, very worried.

After a night on the town it was no simple matter to load Lily into the Chevy. It took the three of us plus two lab assistants to force her into the confines of the bags. She was brawny and violent. Her hooves had a way of slashing through the burlap, and at the sound of her voice, windows opened up and down the street. But finally she was stuffed into the trunk of the Chevy and a crack left open when the lid was lashed down to provide her with refreshing drafts of carbon monoxide.

Once under way, she stopped kicking and fussing, ostensibly soothed by the motion. Unfortunately, we had to stop for lights often, and then she screamed like a soul at the gates of hell. Motorists stared, peering with shocked faces into our seemingly empty car, wondering whether they were hearing cries of help from a kidnapped victim of the Mafia. Some even looked under our wheels, expecting that we had just run over some innocent bystander. They were disconcerted to find nothing — no mutilated corpse — nothing. At any moment we expected to hear police sirens; Fran gunned the motor at each red light, prepared for a quick getaway. Luckily, murders are not the agenda of traffic cops, and they paid no attention to us.

By the time we were out of the city, we were rigid with the strain of appearing so respectable, and so deaf. We didn't relax until we drove into the barnyard. It took Uncle Bill, Newt, Fran, Wayland, the chore boy and a couple of obliging boarders to wrestle Lily into her pen. Once there, she forgot her traumatic ride and set to work eating. Day by day she ripened, became mountainous. Uncle Bill hung over the fence making comforting sounds and feeding her succulent bits usually reserved for Ma's favorite cats.

A month later, Duckett called to say that he had made a small error; he had slipped up in his records — he should have taken just one more sample of Lily's blood. But not to worry, he would be up shortly and would bring the equipment needed to tap her once again. By the time he came, armed with a sizeable vial, syringes and ether, Lily had increased by several more pounds and bloomed with rosy health. Duckett reassured Ma and Uncle Bill that getting a bit of blood was nothing. Lily could spare it, wouldn't notice its loss. So one evening after an invigorating round of highballs, the time had come for the job of bloodletting.

The scene was set in the lower stable, under the barn. Behind the row of cows tied up in their stanchions, planks were laid across a pair of sawhorses. Half a dozen interested boarders muscled Lily onto the operating table. Duckett and another doctor wore surgical gowns; the second doctor was assigned the task of applying the ether cone and letting it drip on Lily's twitching nose. Two more assistants held aloft kerosene lanterns. All that was lacking was a Rembrandt to record the scene for posterity.

Lily's eyes soon closed. She wore a smile of conscious virtue and burbled juicily in her dreams.

But now it became apparent that Duckett had never actually performed this chore himself; he couldn't locate a vein beneath Lily's fat. Kibitzers pointed out likely spots for puncturing with no success. Every few minutes somebody would call for more ether. The fumes of whiskey and ether were making everyone groggy. Lily's pulse became slower and slower, and finally quit. Her etherized soul ballooned up, up — and away.

Duckett looked disconcerted. Uncle Bill looked downright ferocious. Lily looked angelic. Now there was no longer any difficulty in finding a vein; Lily was opened up and the vial was filled. The operating crew wove their way back upstairs and poured themselves restorative drinks.

Next day Duckett went back to Boston satisfied that even if all had not gone exactly to plan, at least he had his sample, and Ma and Uncle Bill had their pork. But no, it didn't work out all that well. Lily's meat was so saturated with ether that it had to be destroyed.

It took all of Duckett's charm, all his powers of persuasion to mollify Ma after such a debacle, but none of that worked with Uncle Bill. Ever thereafter if Duckett's name was so much as mentioned in his presence, Bill would twist his face into a grimace as though he smelled something bad. Like ether.

❧ Baked Beans? Oh, Then It's Saturday

THOSE weekends with bird shooters or skiers were all-absorbing, charged-up periods. It was like riding the rapids in an overloaded boat: exciting, fun, with no allowances made for rocks and shoals. There were no life jackets, no reserve supplies. Emergencies were faced when they happened. If food ran out, Ma coped. On a farm, even a poor farm, there was always something still in the henhouse or in a bin down cellar.

It's doubtful if Ma had ever been to a hotel, and she had seldom gone to a restaurant. She had no idea how such places were run and made no attempt to learn. Instead of planning standard menus, she made them up as she went along, often to suit her own moods. "Mabel, I feel like having dandelion greens today — is there any salt pork? Look in the cellar, in that crock near the washtubs."

When Mabel arrived each morning, she had no idea in what direction she would be heading that day. She and Ma battled their way through each suggested dish. By late afternoon, Mabel often resembled a scow in heavy seas with all her seams about to burst. But there was always Saturday to look forward to — Saturday was the one day with a firm schedule: baked beans and brown bread, a port in the storm.

Just because her business had grown out of all proportion, Ma saw no reason to invest in more equipment; she made do. Her "staff" (that was us) could make out somehow. We lugged in cots from the camps, broken springs, hair mattresses and all. There were plenty of blankets purchased at sales and auctions over the years. Ma boasted that she only bought blankets of real wool; if so, the wool must have been from mastodons, oxen or yaks. Those blankets were bonecrushers. By morning guests were worn out from their weight.

Monday was Wash Day. Even if there were forty sheets, Ma rejected the new-fangled notion that sheets could be done by a Laundry. Mabel valiantly strove to accomplish the impossible, and by Monday night sheets were strung on a clothesline across the front porch. If a boarder stayed on through Monday, not only could he not see out the front window, but because the sheets blocked out any ray of sun, the living room was bathed in a dismal, cold-sheet light. But Monday was Monday, and Ma was consistent about Mondays. What nearly broke her spirit and forced her to send the sheets out was the weather. In freezing weather, the sheets wouldn't dry between weekends.

Occasionally, when we hoped Ma was preoccupied, Fran and I made an attempt to shift furniture about to minimize some of the more uncomfortable hazards. We released a bureau that was jammed up tight between a bed and the wall, because the drawers couldn't be opened except by standing on the bed. Mabel tattled, and we had to put it back. Ma was displeased; that bureau, she said, was a priceless antique and not meant to be *used*.

The upstairs bathroom was nothing but a slot under the eaves with scant space for a wash basin and toilet, but that was where Ma had elected to keep her sewing machine, an ancient treadle affair that stood in a corner preventing the door from opening all the way. Each time a person came in, the door struck the machine a blow, jarring its joints but keeping them from atrophying.

There was little danger of that anyhow, because no matter whether the farm was stuffed to the roof with guests, when Ma needed something mended, Mabel would be sent up and the bathroom would be put to use. Ma didn't believe in throwing away "perfectly good sheets," even if they were split down the middle. Mabel rehabilitated them on the machine by bringing the two outer edges together in the center, making a strong, corrosive seam through the middle of a boarder's most sensitive regions. To do this, Mabel had to pull the machine away from the wall and set her chair in the doorway, hunch down with her nose practically under the needle (her eyesight was poor) and set stoically to work. Anyone seized with a compulsion to use the bathroom was blocked off; he would have to sprint for the privy in the barn.

"— *Why* is the machine there? I'll tell you why — because it's always been there, that's why." So the bureau stayed where it always had been, and the sewing machine stayed where it was, and Ma continued, "If you've nothing better to do than change things all about for no reason, you might as well be useful. Fran, why can't you fix that window in the north room. Somebody has forced it open — imagine! Why that window hasn't been opened for thirty years, and now all of a sudden somebody thinks they need fresh air . . . fresh air indeed!"

In the middle of the week, all problems were discussed at the noonday meal. Ma didn't worry about problems, she just picked them out of the air and dropped them before us.

"What do we do with the Fultons, first they said there would be *three* of them, and now . . . Mabel! Bring in some of that piccalilli we made yesterday, it would be good with these leftover baked beans . . . now, the Fultons say they're going to be *four* — can you think of another bed anywhere?"

While we were considering this, Ma said, "Mrs. Osterhouse phoned, said she'd left an imported pink angora sweater a few weeks ago. Well, Mabel had found it, but since it had been left like that, we fixed it up to make a nice bed for Pookycat. It's too bad she didn't call about it sooner. Now Pooky's had her kittens in it, and I don't think it looks just right any more." She went on placidly, "Aren't these beet greens delicious — and another thing, Fran, some man called, I didn't get his name, said he'd lost his right shoe. He said *you'd* know where it was — why would you know? Did you see him go hopping off on his left foot? By the way, have any of you seen my needle lately?" (Ma had one needle and one spool of thread.) "I can't find it anywhere. It seems to me I had it when I was reading that letter from Cousin Sally, you don't suppose it could have slipped into the envelope . . . did you look there, Mabel? It wasn't? I wonder if it could have fallen into that basket I keep letters in . . . "

So all hands turned out to look for the needle in Ma's haystack of envelopes. It was found, not there, but in the hem of a skirt she had been mending.

"Well — that's a relief, I did hate to show up at the Ladies Aid this afternoon without my sewing things."

CHAPTER SIX

◆ᳯ *Ladies Aid*

W HEN MA was about to set forth to a meeting of the Ladies Aid at the Parsonage, she had to choose which of her knitting bags she'd take to carry her needle in. She had an impressive collection because friends and boarders were always bringing her new ones, knowing she loved them almost as much as chocolates. Each new bag was supposed to replace an old one, but Ma was loyal to her possessions and could never bear to throw any away, so bags hung like bats from the walls of her sitting room on hooks, nails or spikes.

"Mabel — where is that prescription, Help for Your Acid Stomach, the one Olive gave me? It could be in the bag she brought back from Florida, the one with the roses?"

Mabel came in with the bag. "Here it is, but these aren't roses, they're blue!"

"Well, they look more like roses than anything else, don't they? They aren't *daisies*! Well, then, they're roses. Is that prescription in it?"

"No. And it's not from Florida, either. It has a tag right on it, says 'Made by the North Carolina Craftsmen,' and here's a pamphlet from the Turkish Missionary Society."

"Oh, good! Now I do remember Bessie giving those out at our meeting last spring, and I always meant to read it. But there's no prescription? Look in that other bag, that sort of Mexican thing Jane Lorimer gave me, it's probably under the hot water bottle in my bedroom."

"There's nothing in that Mexican thing, but I brought this orange one; it's got something in it — oh, it's a pattern for crocheted baby pants!"

"Baby pants? Now whatever would I be doing with that! But I suppose it could have been when we decided to make a layette for Ruthie's baby, remember?"

"Yes, I remember, that was for last year's baby, and this year's baby is due any minute."

"Well, who can be expected to keep up with that sort of thing, throw it away — no . . . wait now, don't throw it away, it might just come in handy. Put it back in that bag so we'll know where it is." The handbag went back on its hook under the hot water bottle.

"And now, Mabel, where's my needle?"

Ma's needle was a big coarse affair suitable for making braided rugs. Some of hers turned out well and were durable in spite of the fact that she lavished little care on their construction. Rug-making brought out the adventurer in Ma; she took chances with ingredients as she never did with her baking. She gambled on freakish colors and sewed the braids together with great, looping stitches, unconcerned whether they would hold or not. Some did, but some were jinxed from the start.

For instance, there was a rug in her sitting room that would never lie down properly. She had had Mabel dye an old pair of Wayland's pants a hideous magenta (she said it was *red*, and, if *she* said it was red — then it *was* red). These braided strips did not fit well with the other strips of braided wool; they just did not integrate. And since Ma had started the rug with the magenta in its very center, the result was a bulgy island rising up to trip the unwary. Ma assumed this to be a minor flaw, a mere trifle easily solved by the passing tread of boarders, until the day that it brought old Mrs. Hill crashing down with a full cup of tea in her hand. After that, as a concession, Ma did let Mabel place a card table over it, upside down, legs in the air, and visitors facing Ma on her blue couch had to chat through this inhospitable barrier. After what seemed like a suitable length of time, the table was removed — and, lo, magenta boiled up as obstructive as ever. Undefeated, Ma accepted the challenge and slapped another rug over it, weighed down by a group of four flatirons. (Underneath, magenta bided its time.)

Ma and Mabel were staunch members of the Ladies Aid, a sturdy grey-and-white association dedicated to deeds of benevolence; it was their club. At the opening of every meeting the ladies stood, hands pressed over cotton bosoms, to recite the Pledge, dedicating hearts of purity to deeds of benevolence. This over with and shelved, they got down to the main purpose of the meeting: preparing articles to be sold for local charities. Sheltered behind good intentions they had the time of their lives. The Ladies Aid satisfied a need to meet for friendship, for mutual support, for woman-talk — and as most came from boiled-potato lives, a need for color, for tassels, for embroidery, for elegant rosettes of brilliant yarn. Together they worked to create quilts or rugs so effective they could be hung on walls as decorations. Patches and knitted squares were combined to charm the eye and lighten the heart. Not one of these women could sing, but in each was hidden a note of woolly music bursting to get out.

All took Ma's lack of sewing expertise in stride, quietly grateful that her rugs were not for their annual sale but for home consumption. She had her own niche, and was held in reserve to be brought into play at their annual Ladies Aid

Baked Bean Supper, when smells from her hot crocks of beans and mountains of fresh rolls would draw customers into their net.

Here Ma was at her best; she used no freakish ingredients and spared no pains (she spared none of Mabel's, either).

⋖ Cora and Morris

THE ONLY open space in the center of Nelson was made when the general store, a large brick and granite building (STOVES FEATHERS GRAIN) had burned down, and the cellar hole was filled in to make a Town Common. The houses circled it, sheds and barns almost touching each other. The Town Hall had no parking space (hitching posts had once filled the bill), and the schoolhouse was so close that there was no playground. Not having allowed for growth, Nelson had obligingly shrunk instead.

Cora and Morris's house faced the Common. To reach the Parsonage, Cora had only to skirt their one-horse pasture and cross the church lawn. A short walk, but no distance was easy for her. Cora had to stop to breathe every few steps. She was emaciated; her dress hung from shoulders as narrow as wire coat-hangers. Sizzling blue eyes, a thin, bright nose and over-red cheekbones were signs of the fever that was consuming her lungs. What Cora lacked in bulk and strength, she made up for in determination. If she had really wanted to get to the Ladies Aid meeting on the dot she could have allowed the extra time, but she never did. Somehow she was always just too late to take the Pledge, knowing that it might cramp her style. She always had a good excuse prepared though she had no need, as the ladies gave her credit for coming at all.

"Oh my Saints — is there a chair left? Good! I thought I might as well get rid of the slut's wool under the couch before

I came over," — she stopped to gasp a minute — "but the mop wouldn't reach way back under and me down on my knees and no way to get up, it's a wonder I'm not there yet. Next time I aim to have Morris do it — no trouble him getting *down*, but would he get *up*, seeing as how it's so restful down there and the view so good and all." She took time to ease her lungs and to take account of those present.

Seeing that prim Bessie's attention was distracted and the coast clear for a bit of gossip, she continued, "Maggy not here today? Thought not. Willy must have gone to town to see if he can sell that real old plate Maggy turned up with her cultiva-tor — could be worth something. Soon as he was out of sight, I think I saw Jason streaking up to Maggy's — he's quick that way, is our Jason . . . "

"Well now, Cora, Willy must know what's what . . . he must know . . . "

"Oh no! Not him, why should he? You never miss a slice off a cut loaf, do you?"

Gossip like this was off-limits, frowned upon, but Cora was irrepressible, and they gave her her head. Anyway, they had come to count on her to add that something extra to meetings already guaranteed to lift their spirits up and out of the primal ooze of domestic boredom.

During the war, the women set aside frivolous pieces and concentrated on work for the Red Cross. Such a project was in train when I went to get Ma and Mabel late one afternoon. For a restrained, genteel group they seemed to be in quite an uproar. Broad backs were bent over the table, voices were raised in dissension. Pink-and-white flannel was everywhere — the floor was covered with scraps, and pins had fallen like pine needles in a gale. A sample hanging on the back of a chair revealed that the work in progress was pajamas — men's pajamas for the Veterans' Hospital. The Ladies had hit a snag; they had run aground head on.

At the head of the long table, Cora was reading directions from the pattern sheet. She was agitated, her snow-white hair disordered, her face overflushed. She was the co-ordinating official whose subordinates were in turmoil. Discipline was thrown to the winds along with everything else; threads snarled, scissors clashed.

"That can't be right! Can't you see that's upside down?" Cora waved a frantic hand. "How could it work upside down, I ask you!" She turned back to the directions. "It says here, lay the upper flap on the right-hand side — Mabel, can't you tell which is the right-hand side? Just hold it up in front of you and use your right hand . . . yes, like that . . . well, no — not like that — he'd have to be left-handed. Oh, Sadie, you're making the opening over a foot long, whoever heard of a — well, never mind." She studied the sheet again. "Now, turn the flap to the front of the left side opening and stitch neatly along the edge . . . which is the edge — where *is* the edge?" She stood up to get a view down the whole length of the table.

"Sarah, you're doing it on the backside — the man would have to be an acrobat . . ." Coughing, she sat down hurriedly, then, putting her handkerchief to her mouth, she coughed in terrible spasms.

The women threw down their scissors, dropped all the pieces and went to her aid. It was decided to get her home immediately, and the meeting broke up.

They took her home and went in to settle her on her couch, to cover her with her favorite "african," to calm the distressed and flustered Morris. It was urged that a doctor be called, but the suggestion frightened Cora and she protested in frantic gasps, "No — no! I won't have the doctor. I'll be — all right — in a bit. Morris, get my pills — beside the sink."

They didn't call the doctor, and Sarah offered to watch through the night. Not only Cora, but Morris had to be cared for. They all knew, because they would have done the same, that if her husband were not provided with a hot dinner, Cora would drag herself up even if it brought on a hemorrhage.

Half asleep, half delirious during the dark hours of difficult and shallow breathing, Cora had a vision. A vision of an angel who hovered over her with slowly beating wings. A feather drifted down, a feather of pink-and-white flannel, a narrow strip that fluttered and eddied about in a wayward fashion. Soon more and more feathers fell until, she claimed later, she was near smothered.

"That angel," she declared, "had a real bad case of the molt."

Over the next few days, the women took turns at Cora's. They pushed Morris into activity, told him to feed the hens, made poultices and watched till Cora could move about without coughing her lungs out. She got better — not well, she would never be well — but well enough so she could at least get to the next Ladies Aid.

Returning from a meeting, Cora could count on finding her house just as she expected. In a slump. Morris would be in the rocking chair by the kitchen stove, boots off and feet resting on the open oven door; the fire out, newspapers spread all over the floor, a grey dredging of tobacco ash down his shirt front and peppering the fur of the yellow cat on his lap, an empty beer bottle standing beside him on the floor. Hearing Cora's step, Morris would slip one foot from the oven door and inch the bottle under the stove and out of sight.

As soon as she could get her breath, Cora would set up her customary caterwauling and begin to slam pots and pans about. Still, mellowed by an uplifting meeting and still under the benign influence of Christian tolerance, she usually didn't throw anything.

By the time Morris had scuffled up the papers and jammed them into the stove to start the fire, she had simmered down and was able to gasp, "In a minute or two — I'll heat up the hash . . . do you want an egg on it? Where's that broom you promised to bring back from the barn? Did you feed the hens? And how about that trash on the back porch. You left it there, and now you can pick it up!"

All this was routine, repetition practiced and comfortable. She pitched, and he either dodged or let the shots bounce off his hide. A break in the expected pattern was disturbing. But it happened.

Morris had no car and didn't want one. His horse and buggy got him around well enough at a speed in keeping with his chosen life-style as a handyman for several families, doing a little of this and a little less of that. He and his horse were kindred souls. Bowed with toil, they both carried their heads low, lifted their feet just high enough to clear the ground, and were caught by surprise at any small rise, such as a pebble. Once or twice a month, he, and Cora if she was able, made a trip to Keene on the "stage" (the mailman's station wagon) to stock up on supplies. The rest of the time, Morris would drive the three miles to the small store for everyday necessities — baking soda, a couple of pounds of soldier beans, crackers and, naturally, beer and tobacco.

The store was to the men what the Ladies Aid was to the women, a meeting place, a stamping ground. Here they gathered to complain of the weather, to compare notes on mealworms or potato bugs, to slander the Selectmen or the Democrats. There were chairs set out along the porch of the store, and the men would drag out doing the errands for an hour or so.

Any hint from Cora that she was running short of matches or pins and Morris would instantly offer to go to the store. Supper would be cold before he made it home. Coming back, the horse slept along on its feet while Morris, relaxed, put his head back to pour beer down his throat, his eyes following the pattern of treetops overhead.

After one such trip, Morris seemed stunned by some unmentionable ordeal. He stopped eating. He refused to go to the store. He would stare at Cora beseechingly, his mouth opening as if he were about to explain, but then it would snap shut again. He was a pitiful sight, sitting on the back porch, twisting his hands together, distraught, obviously beset by some mental anguish. He wouldn't even go near the beer he kept stashed in the henhouse.

Cora was alarmed. Convinced that he was in a decline, sickening for something, she stopped yelling at him, and reviewed her store of cure-alls. Drastic medication was called for. She had just begun to prepare a stimulating pick-me-up of equal parts of syrup of rhubarb, paregoric and spirits of camphor when he was saved by the mail.

He trudged out to the group of mailboxes at the edge of the Common to get the newspaper. Opening it on the way back to the house, he stood stock-still for a minute and then continued at a shambling trot, calling out, "Cora — see, it was true! I *did* see a monkey — says so right here in the paper — look! 'MONKEY CAPTURED — A monkey which had escaped from a traveling show was found in the wood near Nelson Village . . . ,' and I seen it as plain as plain . . . I knew all the while it couldn't be the beer! I seen it, and I couldn't tell nobody — just nobody — they'd have said I was polluted . . . "

Morris was restored. Back to normal, he went to the store and sat on the porch for hours, a can of beer in one hand and the newspaper in the other. He showed it to all the summer people he chored for and wouldn't listen when they tried to tell him where to pile the kindling or suggested that he rake the grass. He was a new man.

Cora was so relieved that she cooked him a great mess of his favorite food, fried tripe. And when he got sick from overeating, she gave him that mixture of rhubarb, paregoric and camphor she had all ready and right on hand.

೪ The Hot Line

IT WAS ABOUT noon one day when Sarah came down the road. The boarders were waiting on the porch for word that lunch was ready, and Fran and Wayland were in the barn doorway. Sarah was a little stick of a woman, tired and dusty, carrying a bunch of ferns and wilted daisies in her hand to brush away the flies. She was on her way to "help out" a neighbor and had another mile to go. Fran was particularly relieved at her appearance, as he could see with his own eyes that her sister hadn't chopped her up to feed the hens.

He needn't have worried; Sarah would never have allowed herself to be chopped unless she were positive that was the Lord's Will. With Him she was in constant communication. She was old, worn out, half-starved, but didn't know it; that was her strength. She hadn't a clue that she was decrepit, over the hill, so she just kept trotting through life, limping sometimes, carrying out the order of the day as prescribed from Higher Up.

She only came to the Ladies Aid when she was convinced that they were doing the Lord's work. Those pajamas, for instance, were for Christian soldiers fighting against the powers of evil; and if putting in those flies hindside-to was in aid of that cause, Sarah could be counted on to do her bit. She was the one who invariably stayed to clean up after the Ladies

Aid supper; she was the garbage-pail scrubber, the cupboard washer-upper, all done with smiling good will. It was she who had offered to spend a sleepless night watching over Cora. To the women in town she was a blessing, maybe more — maybe she was a saint, if the definition of "saint" is one who is pious, tirelessly helpful and a bit simple.

"Why, there's Sarah!" said Wayland. He huffed himself up and out and took her hand. She was obviously exhausted, having already walked three miles from her home. He went on, "Come in and rest a minute — it's hot — and have a bite to eat."

"Why, yes indeed," she said as Wayland helped her up the steps, she would be glad to stop by for a minute, but just for a glass of water. She had no need, she said, for nourishment; she had eaten before leaving home. And no doubt she had, if she said so — Sarah would never lie. A place was hastily set for her, and as she sat down, she smiled to right and left and bowed her head in silent grace — then daintily put away a man-sized helping of pot roast, potatoes, carrots and a large piece of pie.

Afterwards she insisted on taking the dishes out to the kitchen. As she took her leave, she gave Ma the bunch of wilted daisies. (She had her pride, and when accepting a favor always gave something in return.) Wayland drove her to her destination, where she would clean for an hour or two and be driven back with her earnings plus some new bread and vegetables, which would keep her and her sister going for a while.

Clearing up in the kitchen, Ma said, "Mabel, you can put the potato peels into the hens' kettle."

"There aren't any peels."

"Mabel! Of course there are peels."

"No, there aren't — there's not one single peel."

And there wasn't. Sarah had swept them all into her

pocket. Ma was put out. The whole episode put her out. In the first place, Wayland had stolen her thunder by extending an invitation — invitations were *her* prerogative. And secondly, she was affronted by Sarah's taking the peels; she felt that somehow it was a slur on her generosity. "Did she think I'd begrudge her a few peels, for heaven's sakes . . . !"

It was more likely that while Sarah was in the kitchen and that pile of peels right there, Word had come down to her through the Divine antenna — "It is a Sin to waste the fruits of the earth." And Sarah had seen her duty.

If Sarah was the epitome of a meek and gentle saint, her sister, Lizzie, though equally religious, was quite, quite different.

Lizzie was a militant Christian; she saw herself as the hand of the Lord, with a sacred obligation to strike down sinners, to quell the wicked, to bring them to their knees with thunder and bolts of lightning. She scorned Sarah's mild ways. But Sarah was impervious, safe behind her blinders of faith.

Tall, gaunt, iron-chinned Lizzie stalked the roads, sometimes on a pilgrimage to save souls, sometimes to sell some article she had made at home in the dark of the moon. One year it was balsam pillows. At least, she called them pillows. They were made from garish, shiny pink nylon bloomers, stuffed malevolently hard with needles, obscene and carcass-colored. Anyone intimidated into buying one had to slip out in the dead of the night and bury it in the woods, looking back over his shoulder and trembling at the hoot of an owl.

On a night of violent wind, the sisters' dilapidated old barn fell down. Next morning Lizzie in a high old temper strode over to a neighbor's and called for a State Trooper. She shouted, "An emergency? Certainly it's an emergency!" She was waiting in front of the house, taut and belligerent, when the Trooper arrived in an official car with blue revolving lights, State insignia — the works. She pointed to the wrecked barn. "THAT is the work of the Devil. He flew in a plane so low we could hear the flap of its wings. Now — DO something!"

The Trooper opened his door and got out, massive, immaculate, badge gleaming with authority. He examined the towering pile of weathered boards, the caved-in roof, the tufts of rotten hay drifting down. He exchanged hard looks with a dusty rooster squatting high where the loft once had been. Walking around slowly, he stood where he could see the bits of machinery protruding, the busted wheels and cracked shafts all jumbled together like a giant squirrel's nest. He strode back to Lizzie, and getting out a black notebook and pencil, he wrote down the date. Shaking his head grimly, he turned to her. "Madame, you're quite right. You do have a disaster — I think I would go so far as to describe it as a disaster of *major proportions*. The matter will be reported to headquarters, and you may rest assured that action will be taken."

Lizzie was gratified and watched him depart, confident that the problem had been placed in the best hands. She was so relieved that she put it completely out of her mind. After all, she had other problems, other fleas in her bonnet. There were those *bootleggers* to cope with.

She was beset by bootleggers, bootleggers who sneaked about at night, hiding in bushes, lurking in old sheds. Bootleggers who had kidnapped the foster boy that she and Sarah had taken in out of the goodness of their hearts, to lead him along the paths of righteousness. And he had taken off, vanished. Just how the boy had come into their hands is unknown, but as he grew older, it all got too much for him — too many prayers and too little food. He left, but Lizzie knew that he had not left of his own accord; he had been kidnapped and was perhaps being held captive by bootleggers somewhere in her woods. She raged around behind the house, slashing at bushes with a great stick, breathing fire, yelling threats of retribution. Then she remembered that helpful State Trooper, and put in another call.

Surprisingly, he came again and courteously listened to her complaints. Hand on revolver, he reconnoitered the house, Lizzie by his side, now and then hollering, "Come out with your hands up!" Silence. Lizzie was reassured, she calmed down, she offered him a glass of lemonade. Sarah, in her own world where violence didn't exist, kept out of sight.

(It may have been Sarah's hot line to heaven that brought the trooper in answer to these emergency calls. His visits were subsidized by either the State or the Lord, and were successful — but who should get the credit?)

Thanks to him, Lizzie's forays slowed down. She became reconciled to the absence of the foster boy, to the drifting away of bootleggers from her bailiwick. The scrub and alders, the weeds and blueberry bushes thrashed and broken down, were left to recuperate, though she continued to stand motionless in the devastated area she had created, her head cocked, listening for signs of the enemy. If she heard no suspicious sounds, she went about her business, hoeing the garden patch, or preparing wood for the kitchen stove, which she did by snatching up a piece of board, taking it to the chopping block and beating it to death.

But Lizzie's militant nature couldn't be subdued permanently. Her religious energy demanded opposition; she needed fields to conquer. Starting a new phase, she turned against her mild and gentle sister. Lizzie despised mildness, to her a form of religious sloth. She grumbled that Sarah shirked, she lacked moral force, she was not aggressive in pursuing the Lord's work or tussling with the devil.

"Good for nothing, that's what she is — useless, worthless!" she'd mutter to herself as she viciously split kindling with a wildly swinging axe. "Chop her up! Chop her up — that's what I've a mind to do — food for the hens, that's all she's good for . . ."

Fran, who had seen her in action with the axe, feared that she might be capable of it if she had the impulse. He was a Selectman at the time and felt some responsibility — was Lizzie becoming dangerous or not? Should she be under observation? Seeking advice, he called the State Hospital and told them the story. The doctor in residence listened patiently and asked, "Has she actually attacked her sister?"

"No," said Fran, "not yet."

"Ah, well, in case she does, be sure to give us a ring." Fran had to be content with that. So he was always relieved when he passed Sarah's bent little figure trotting along on one of her missions to clean up someone's kitchen, still smiling, still wearing the same flowered hat. As she never did receive word from On High that she should offer herself as a sacrifice for the hens, she made herself unavailable when Lizzie had a go with the axe.

Lizzie's crusading days came to an abrupt halt when she overextended herself and blew a fuse. She crumpled. From then on, she was no longer seen striding about, brandishing her stick. Sarah stayed home to care for her, the Ladies left a standing order for groceries to be delivered to their door, and the Selectmen hired Morris to provide wood. Characteristically, the Town kept its distance but watched over them.

Some time later, Fran and I returned from a long spell away visiting my family to find the sisters gone.

It had happened during an epidemic of the flu. There was

a storm of whirling purple winds and singing turbulence, and during the night of flashing blackness the Lord's hand swooped down like a great vacuum cleaner and inhaled them both.

❧ The Brick Schoolhouse

WHEN MA was teaching at the Nelson school before she married Wayland, she received this letter from the mother of one of her pupils. She kept it in a basket under a cat, along with a couple of newspaper clippings (a Sermon and an article on Hen Lice), a buttonhook, two packages of cucumber seed and some lace.

Dear Miss French,

Georgie has a terrible cough and it is hardly prudent to let him out today, but we dislike to have him lose any time from school, and will you oblige him to stay in the schoolroom, I mean not to go out playing, and also see that he wears his overcoat home buttoned up, he is so careless, and that he does not sit in a draught. He coughed 2½ hours last night without one minute's rest. Mr. B. would have gone for the Dr. in a half-hour if he had not stopped. We gave him Adamson's Balsam-Spruce gum syrup, syrup of epicac [sic], Warren's troche-potash tablets, ginger and molasses, hot mustard-water flannels and catarrh stuff. At last Leslie held his hands around Georgie's throat and got it to sweating and he finally went to sleep. Please try to make him be careful, and oblige

Mrs. Bidwell

Our son Barry was a restless five when we eagerly enrolled him in the same school. We didn't know or care whether the school was good or not, or what standards it had — any school would have done at that point. Fran and Newt had both gone there, along with lots of other Tolmans, and none of their lives had been wrecked. Besides, I hoped that the taint of having a mother "from the outside" would be reduced if Barry were tossed into the common pot. Of course, he was born a native anyway, but my own position might be improved if as his mother I could attack local prejudice at the level of the first grade — the soft underbelly of the town.

When a new child came to the school, the girls took him over. They helped him off with his coat and overshoes, wiped his nose and introduced him to his desk. And if it happened that the child, terrified and homesick, spent the first days wailing continuously, one of the girls was always beside him, patting, crooning words of comfort and mopping (often more than just tears).

During the winter, snow was tracked in by the students, making the atmosphere damp, steamy and pungent as many of the boys came to school right from the cow barn. The stove was dominant. The Town provided wood, and it was the job of the biggest, toughest boys to split it to size in the entryway. They fought among themselves for the honor of wielding the axe. They chopped everything that came their way and in their enthusiasm they even reduced to kindling a parlor organ brought from upstairs and left to be repaired. The plank floor was chipped and battered.

The privy was a lean-to attached to the back of the buildings. At the rear of the schoolroom there was a door for the girls, but no inside door for the boys; they had to dash out the front and around to the back. To my suburban standards, this seemed a little rugged for a five year old, but Barry was scornful of my fussing. "Naw, that's nothing, what's a little cold . . .," he stopped and considered. "Well, maybe one thing

— some of the boys get kind of careless, and I hate sitting on all that ice."

At the time the schoolhouse was built, the Selectmen were all Deacons of the Church, and the building exemplified rectitude: upright, strong as a fort, made to last. And it would have, had it not been for children. Like the church, the schoolhouse had two doors, one for each sex; it was once assumed that unless segregation was established there would be hanky-panky. By now, however it had once been, the children were simply separated into classes. (There was only one other child in Barry's class, forcing him to be either at the top or the bottom.) All eight grades — when there were enough children for eight grades — were in the first-floor room. The second floor was the Concert Hall, off-limits except for the annual Exercises put on by the teacher to expose parents to the talents of their young. At these affairs, the teacher played the piano (the organ having come to a sad end), and the children sang strangled songs in an incomprehensible jargon.

The Selectmen assumed that a school had one purpose: education. Other activities could take place at home or anywhere else; they were not the concern of the taxpayers. Playing was not part of the curriculum. Recess was for the purpose of getting the kids out of the teacher's hair for a blessed half hour. She didn't supervise them; they were to get *out* — what they did there was not her business. There was no "play equipment," except for the children's own sticks and balls with which they could either fight or play baseball, it was up to them. In snowy weather, the steep hill leading to the school made for good sliding and the kids careened down in dishpans brought from home, ending up in tangled, screaming heaps.

If the weather was bad — very, very bad — they had to stay in.

During the dark days of February, the girls colored end-less sheets of paper, but the boys stood about, morose, frus-trated by the lack of action. They craved adventure, some goal to pursue in their spare time, preferably something danger-ous, or at least illegal. They had nothing to occupy themselves with but lugging logs from the woodpile outside to the storage place under the staircase. This repetitious job had to be done every day.

One day a boy amused himself by weaseling in behind the wood under the stairs and managed to shove some logs around so as to make a hollow next to the outer wall. He backed himself in and found he had a cosy, secret spot. He wished it weren't so dark. Scrabbling with his fingers, he found some crumbling mortar and worked at it futilely — he needed a tool. Wriggling back out, he bumped into another boy who asked eagerly, "Whatcher doing back there — find a rat?"

"Sh-h-h, stupid! Shut up!" And right then and there a conspiracy was born.

Together the boys pulled and shoved to enlarge the space so that by taking turns they could work a brick loose and let in some light. First they used a fork stolen from home, and later when they had elbow room, the axe. They kept the wood piled high in front as a protective screen, and assigned one boy as sentinel. Soon they became more ambitious; they would make this an escape hatch, a secret passage from their imagi-nary prison. Although all this wasn't exactly fraught with danger, at least it was a project that called for devious plotting, for silence on pain of death. Day by day, during bad weather, they hacked away and finally broke a hole all the way through. A triumph! A boy squeezed out and was free, free by his own efforts. To him, it had it all over simply opening the front door and tamely going out.

Eventually somebody tattled, the School Board got wind of it, the boys were bawled out and the hole re-bricked. Next year, they had to start all over again.

Now that I had a vested interest in the school, when there was an opening on the School Board, I volunteered, hoping to bolster my position in town and also quite curious about how things were run, if they were. I got the job; nobody else wanted it. During my three-year term, I was a model member. I suggested no improvements, kept my mouth shut and never mentioned what I thought of the boys' privy.

The last year of my term I did make one contribution. It had to do with the Lavery children. They didn't show up during sugaring, or spring planting, or apple-picking time, or when the potatoes had to be dug or the fishing was good. The Board felt it their bounden duty to do something about this, but they were all terrified of Mrs. Lavery, an ogress who chewed up and spat out anyone who opposed her. To avoid confrontation, they decided that their first move would be to send her a Stiff Letter. If that didn't work, they would threaten her with the Truant Officer (not that we had one). By rotation, I was by this time the Head Member, and also the most expendable, as my term would be up first, so I was assigned the task of composing the letter.

I approached this assignment with qualms. One wrong statement, the Board warned, and Mrs. Lavery would offer to sue, and the last thing we needed was to be faced with a lawyer.

First, I went to the County Educational Headquarters and got a copy of the laws relating to School Attendance, which we found nearly incomprehensible. Since Fran was then our State Representative and supposedly right up on gobbledy-legalese, I roped him in to interpret. We studied the report minutely, word by word, in order to use it to best effect in the letter. In the end, we quoted statements verbatim, listed bylaws by article and number, wrote and rewrote every loaded sentence. Not one opening could be left that might be misinterpreted, not one phrase that might trap us into a libel suit. Many hours and many headaches later, we typed the letter up meticulously. It was a masterpiece. The other members of the Board checked and rechecked each word once more and eventually signed, looking haggard.

Our first plan had been to mail the letter to avoid confronting Mrs. Lavery in person, but she might well claim that it had never come. So it had to be delivered by hand — by my hand, as Chairman of the Board.

Fran drove me down the road to her house, turned around and parked, headed out. Knocking on the front door, I stepped in, keeping one hand on the doorknob behind me. I held out the official document and began my rehearsed speech, "By the authority of the School Board of the Town of Nel— , " and right then Mrs. Lavery let out a screech of rage and snatched the letter. Without opening it, or so much as glancing at it to see what it was, she tore it to shreds and took a threatening step in my direction. I retreated, she lunged and I bolted for the car. Fran had the door open and the motor running, and we shot away with Mrs. Lavery in hot pursuit. The last we saw of her, she was standing in the road, still shrieking, in a drift of shredded paper. Next day, the Lavery children were all in school.

My term on the School Board was a modest success, and having a son in the school helped my relationship with other parents in town, too (at least we had runny noses in common). You couldn't call this a breakthrough exactly; I certainly hadn't cleared that imaginary fence, but at least I had a toehold on the bottom rail. My position was further improved by the encounter with Mrs. Lavery, as, at one time or another, nearly everyone in town had suffered at her hands, so most were both secretly pleased, and secretly sympathetic, that I had not managed to escape humiliation altogether. Still, no one felt comfortable enough to laugh with me to my face.

A toehold on the bottom rail was as far as I ever got. The fence stood firmly in place, never changed — but I did. Gradually I came to accept it, to adapt, and to recognize that the barrier did not exist solely to close me out, but had other roles, other purposes. It provided a deterrent against invasions of all kinds from the outside world, made "togetherness," that dreary state precluding individuality, virtually impossible, sheltered dreams and nourished the shy eccentric. And it was a flexible fence. It didn't prevent the circulation of ideas; through it gusts of friendship could blow freely. I learned to see through it, talk through it, even lean on it.

CHAPTER SEVEN

❧ Moneybags

ALTHOUGH I resigned from the School Board when Barry left the Nelson School, I still wanted to keep a place in town affairs. So, when the office of Town Treasurer became vacant, I applied, ran and was elected, again without opposition. This was another job nobody wanted, even at the starting salary of $35 a year. This kept my finger in the town pie, which wasn't all that full of plums I might add — not that I *could* add, even plums.

The Town Hall had no office space, just the one large room used for the annual Town Meeting and for occasional square dances. The business of the town was carried on from the First Selectman's kitchen, and papers were shuttled back and forth from the Town Clerk's home or the Tax Collector's or the Treasurer's. This allowed for sociability and made it easy to misplace things.

The new Town Treasurer did her job from home, too. It could be done in between things — in between bookbinding, helping out at the farmhouse weekends, taking care of the horses or cleaning camps. A job to fill in those long winter evenings, where in between one set of jobs one did another set of jobs. One day I had an empty hour in between and decided to wash my hair. I had a special rig for hair-washing — an old shirt with the sleeves ripped out and a pair of bedraggled grey flannels kept in the ragbag. An outfit like that invites the unexpected caller. And sure enough there was a knock on the door.

I didn't panic. Often people would drop by asking to buy copies of Fran's block prints, so I answered the door with no qualms. There stood two men with briefcases, wearing hard grey suits, all pressed and buttoned and obviously geared for trouble.

"You are Mrs. Tolman, Treasurer of the Town of Nelson," they stated. I lost my head instantly. Right then I should have said I was out; I looked it and I felt it. "We're Auditors for the state of New Hampshire making a spot check of the Town Accounts." And before I knew it they were in, visitors about as comfortable as two steel posts.

"We'll need your Cash Books, Vouchers and Receipts for the past five years."

"Of course, of course . . . ," I quavered. "I'll get them out for you."

Of course, of course! I had them all right. Of *course* I did. What put me in a swivet was getting them with those two watching. Those accounts were "filed" in a loft at the end of the living room, accessible only by a ladder attached to the wall. The four-foot-high loft had no practical use except as storage room for out-of-date accounts. My custom, over the years, had been to reach up to the loft with a broom, poke open the door and, standing well back, throw the packaged accounts, each dated, labeled and tied with string, as far as I could up into the loft. Then I'd poke the door shut and leave the accounts to the tender care of whatever bats and mice were in residence.

There may be treasurers who can look composed and dignified when climbing up a ladder, but I had not been elected with that in mind. I considered asking the auditors to step outside for a minute, but knew that would look suspicious. So there was nothing for it; I climbed up and rear-ended myself into the loft.

Crawling about on all fours under the eaves, I located each package, stacked them at the entrance and then called down, "Are you ready? Well, then — catch!" And I started pitching as fast and as hard as I could. The first batch caught one auditor off guard and knocked his glasses askew, but after that they showed more talent in fielding.

At floor level, I set up a card table. They took off their coats, got out sheets of columned paper, red pencils, blue pencils, paper clips, staplers — the works. Then, turning back their cuffs to avoid contamination, they got at it.

It took several hours. For a bit I circled about them, offering helpful suggestions. "Can you read those figures all right? That was the year I had poison ivy all up and down my arms. I got it on the Branch River fishing with Fran, so the sums on that page do look sort of scratchy. . ." Another time I tried to explain how a total might appear to be incorrect, but if they turned to the next page it would explain itself. "See, that was because Morris brought his taxes all in coins stuffed in a sack. It took me a couple of days to sort them out and pile them up and so you see that's why it's split up onto two pages."

In vain. Their concentration was so great that they were deaf to my helpful comments; they just kept on checking, drawing lines, comparing figures. I didn't exist. So I drank three cups of coffee and never offered them as much as a glass of water; they probably had no mechanism for swallowing, anyway.

Eventually they aligned, clipped and stapled their way out of the house, leaving me with an official document, all stamped, dated and authorized with illegible signatures and red seals.

The accounts must have proved to be absolutely perfect, else I would have received something nasty and legal from the State, but there was a pleasant silence. The only after-effect of the visitation was that now I never heard a knock at the door without looking for a place to hide.

One of my duties as treasurer was to collect receipts from our Town Clerk, who had a system of bookkeeping as efficient as mine. A widower and a dear little man, he lived alone in a bolt-upright, narrow, scrawny little house. Everyone had to go to him for car registrations and dog licenses. A knock on the door, and he too would be caught off base, scuffling about in his slippers, hurriedly picking up dishes and shoving aside the frying pan to make room on his kitchen table for his account book. Forms were kept in a towering golden-oak sideboard, a masterpiece of wooden spires, pigeonholes and crenellated shelves ornamented with scrollwork, all bursting with papers and wadded accounts. If he were called upon to look up anything that went back more than a year, he'd get flustered and mutter, "Of course — I know just where it is, let me think now. I keep all those records in the other room, you know, so as not to get things mixed up." And off he'd go to his bedroom where, from the open door, one could glimpse a rumpled cot with a hairy dog sprawled across it.

His current receipts were always at hand, he said. He'd put them in the Safe overnight, and he'd fetch them right off. The Town Safe, a huge iron, elaborately decorated antique, was in his barn across the road. So he had to put on his coat, his rubbers and his mittens, the barn doors had to be forced open, the nesting hens brushed off the top of the safe before he could begin the complicated twiddling of the combination.

While I waited, there was the sideboard to study. Shoved

in among the papers on the shelves were many items — bits of candles, candy, patent medicines. A bottle of Glover's Mange Cure had dripped down the face of the sideboard and drooled over a clutch of envelopes fastened with red string.

When the Town Clerk reappeared, and had taken off his coat, mittens and rubbers, we got down to work, going over the checks and cash and adding it all up. It would be correct and his report would be perfect, if slightly marred by eggy smears that the kitchen knife couldn't quite scrape off.

By now, I had gained some confidence in my job, and I began to wonder whether, with all my expertise, I might not be able to lend Ma a hand with her bookkeeping. What a notion!

❧ Accounts and Reckonings

HELP INDEED! She didn't need any help, what was I talking about!

"Well, I could help you balance your checkbook, for instance."

"Pooh," she said, "what nonsense. Last year the bank made a mistake, and now I never do whatever-it-is — balance it — just a waste of time."

"What happened to that check that was lost a month or so ago? Did you notify the bank?"

"Of course not — why would I notify them? After all, they're the bankers, not me . . . it's up to them to know that sort of thing; I shouldn't have to teach them their business . . ."

She had her system, and it worked. When a boarder was ready to leave, he'd come into the kitchen and say, "We're off, Ma. We're all packed up. Have you our bill ready?"

Naturally she didn't have the bill ready — she never gave bills a thought. But now that the subject had come up, it called for a summit meeting, an event, and Ma was prepared to make the most of it. She deliberated. "Your bill? No, it's not quite ready. But I'll get at it if you'll come to my sitting room after I get this cake in the oven. Mabel, have you buttered the pan? Let's see — I'll be there in about fifteen minutes." The boarder had been granted an audience.

Business, important business, wasn't done in the kitchen. It meant moving to her office, the sitting room.

As Ma grew older and her knees got weaker, any move was laborious — took preparation. Mabel was alerted to fetch her cane and stand by. Once on her feet, Ma steadied herself for a minute, notifying her engines that steam would be needed. Tugboat-like, Mabel held herself in readiness with reassuring puffs and grunts, able to supply an expert nudge or supporting bulk when Ma got under way.

Finally, ensconced on her blue couch, settled among her pillows and baskets, Ma was officially ready for business, the boarder seated opposite her.

Now Ma would poke through her baskets for an appropriate scrap of paper. "Would you please just hand me that jar of pens there on my desk? — it's there somewhere, oh yes, behind that vase of irises. Alice is forever bringing me her iris, but I honestly think mine are better than hers . . ." Pen jar found, she took out a fountain pen from the collection, most of which had splayed noses and been useless for a dozen years. Pens defied Ma. The one she'd picked was dry. Chatting away, she selected another, also dry.

"Mabel! Fetch me the ink bottle." Dipping the pen into the sludge at the bottom, she made a try-out blob on a piece of newspaper. Then, to get the pen flowing properly, she jabbed the nib down over and over again till it opened up like a flower in full bloom. When the pen still wouldn't write, she threw it down and, pawing through the basket again, came up with a chewed stub of pencil. Now to business, pencil poised and at the ready.

"Now, let's see, you came Thursday? Oh yes, of course, I remember it was Friday — baked haddock with parsley sauce — well, it's more a boiled-egg sauce, I guess, and I probably added capers. When I order a fish, I always tell them to be sure and give me one with a good bright eye, that way I know it's really fresh. So — now then, you had dinner that day, and what about Saturday?"

After a weekend, these interviews were Ma's reward. She prolonged them as much as possible, going back over each day, each meal step by step, exacting a full quota of compliments. Each nickel was thrashed out, with Ma making a feint here and there about not charging for some extra or other, confident that the boarder would insist on paying the full price. She knew her boarders.

After the boarder had left, Ma would settle back contentedly in her blue nest, folding and refolding the check which was then tucked into some handy envelope, or into her apron pocket, or perhaps into the back of a magazine she was reading.

She never admitted to mislaying a check. No one would ever know that one had disappeared or been lost unless, as sometimes happened when Mabel brought her blue sweater from behind the door, there'd be a triumphant cry, "*There* it is! I knew I'd put that check in a good safe place."

At one time, a check was salvaged from a copy of *The Robe* as it was about to be returned to the lending library. The check had been used as a bookmark. "In *The Robe?*" Well, of *course* that's where it was. I don't go about leaving checks just *anywhere*. Now what page was I at? I really thought I'd finished the whole book . . ." And the check was snatched into her apron pocket.

All Ma's records were kept, all her bookkeeping was done, from that sitting-room couch. Only there were no records, no bookkeeping unless you could count her Line-A-Day Diary, but this consisted entirely of notes on the weather with occasional cryptic notations such as "W.J. P. called today. Cactus bloomed."

She had given up filling in the check stubs, since the bank failed to keep track of checks still outstanding and did such a piffling job. Still, she must have had a computer in her head; she never overdrew.

One time when I was at the bank, a message had been left for me at the teller's wicket — would I please come to the president's office? Seated at his desk and looking as impressive as you'd expect, the president was thumbing through a small stack of checks. When I came in, he rose courteously and, after the ritual greeting, asked, "I thought I heard that your father-in-law died some months ago?"

"Yes, he did."

"Well, er — so it would seem." His voice fell uneasily as if he feared some unknown quicksand through which it was necessary to pick his way with caution. "It's been brought to my attention by my staff of auditors that something unusual — well, to put it bluntly, something *quite* strange has been going on . . . never before . . . ," he cleared his throat and then blurted out, "the thing is, your father-in-law is *still* writing checks."

That wasn't strange. That was Ma. When she took Wayland for her lawful wedded husband, she wasn't half-hearted about it; she'd taken not only him, but his farm, his bank account and his signature.

Fiercely disputed during her lifetime, Ma's business methods were a success. When she and Wayland were both gone, it was found that they had left no unpaid bills, no mortgages, no tricky contracts to be unraveled, no debts. The land they had worked so hard for, the income-producing camps, and best of all, the endless supply of good-quality boarders, were all free and clear. All done by resisting family advice, by an assumption of regal infallibility. All done from that apron pocket, from those cat-infested baskets.

❧ Weather Forecast: Cloudy, Coming Up Fair

THE EXUBERANT growth of the ski business peaked when Ma and Wayland were on the down-cycle of their lives. Ma's seemingly endless energy began to flag, but just when she might have had to face the fact that it was getting to be too much for her, the skiing at Tolman Pond slowed down and eventually came to a halt.

It was inevitable that the giant ski tows would draw off even the most dedicated of Ma's weekend regulars from the pygmy outfit at the farm. Fran and Newt followed along to the great slopes of the White Mountains. They had no intention of playing David to the Goliath of the big resorts and abandoned their own little tow, leaving it on its simple-minded face, busted and useless. They had never counted on the ski business to last forever. They didn't count on anything, much less anything that depended on good weather; on a sunny day a Yankee checks his rain gear. While his right hand is capering about, his left hand is keeping a sharp eye out in case of trouble. The Tolmans had reserves; they had discarded none of their old interests, just set them on a high shelf.

Newt turned his full attention to writing. Up till then he had stuck to magazine articles, but now he published a book, *North of Monadnock*. He concentrated more on his music and developed his tendency for voluble controversy. Fran went back to the series of block prints that he had been working on for years. He had always entertained himself drawing. Before we were married, he had thought of becoming a commercial artist and went to study at the Boston Museum Art School. But the instruction was wasted; it didn't take. If his instructor set him to copying a classic head — say, Socrates — Socrates would show up on Fran's drawing paper looking like Morris brooding over potato bugs. So after a couple of gloriously liberated years in the city, he gave up and came home. For income he took a four-day-a-week job at the State Legislature which still left him time to continue cutting those block prints of his own people, his town life, his neighbors. (Now and then one would bear a faint resemblance to Socrates.) The ski business had been a fluke. It lacked the staying power of a boarding house.

The summer people's loyalty never wavered. Ma's hardy perennials, her high-grade, shatterproof boarders, permanently rooted in their own camps, were now self-feeding, making fewer demands on Ma and Mabel.

It was seldom that there was nobody staying at the farm except between winter and spring. Then the farm was inaccessible, cut off by a mire of mud and ice. Damp, acid air hung over the pond.

Wayland picked this time of year to go about the business of dying. He did it as he had done everything, unostentatiously, in silence. He left a blank spot, an emptiness; now there would be no chilled bowl of arbutus to prove that spring was just around the corner.

Although his death pulled the rug out from under her, Ma was resolute; she didn't let down — and saw that Mabel didn't either. Pre-spring must be gotten through somehow.

Ma tightened everyone's belts. It was hard to sustain the spirits of her household on a steady diet of turnips and parsnips, parsnips and turnips; if she only had a supply of milk and eggs she could have turned out heart-warming, lip-smacking meals. Unfortunately during pre-spring, it was not only the family, but also the cows and hens that went into a slump. The cows dried up, and hens which had been perky creatures bustling about in the summer heat were now hags. They had lost feathers — some were topless and worse yet, some were bottomless. Still, now and then, some courageous hen managed to lay an egg — a perfectly smooth, perfectly shaped egg, its complexion creamy and smooth as any Hollywood starlet's. Granted that it was the hen who had produced this miracle, Ma, as quartermaster in charge of supplies ("Mabel, did you order more chicken grits?"), felt that she was due part of the credit. She had backed the hen with Ma-power every step of the way and bragged, "Not *everybody* can get hens to lay at this time of the year! And this one single egg will go far to improve the rice pudding, make it a lot richer. Just put that can of syrup on the stove to loosen up the sugar at the bottom — it's dark of course, but dark syrup really has the most flavor, it'll be fine with the pudding."

It took time — and everybody's patience, but Spring came at last, saluted with whistles! with flutes! with violets! with eggs! The hens were back on the job.

Looking out the window, past her plants, at the frail new sunshine, at the willow-green by the pond, at the new jonquils just poking up, Ma sighed with contentment. Looking down at the bowl in front of her on the table, she picked out one egg with a knobby kitchen-scarred hand and ran her thumb over the shell. What texture! How elegant it was — not a blemish, not a wrinkle. "Mabel, do take a look at these — aren't they pretty! Come see."

Mabel stumped over, wiping her hands on her apron. "Well, they're OK I guess — look just like everyday old eggs to me."

Everyday indeed! What a put-down — a perfect example of the poor press the egg has always gotten. "He was left with egg on his face," for instance — why not squash on his face? And when a play fails the critics are bound to say that the author "laid an egg." Laying an egg *should* be high praise — a triumph — ask any hen. To Ma the egg was faultless in design and a symbol of riches — rich custards, pies, omelets.

Far away in a distant country there was another who also held the egg in high esteem — Fabergé; he not only admired but glorified eggs, he set them on pedestals. As a Master Craftsman in Russia he was called upon to create works of art for royalty. These might have been in any form, but he selected to make them as eggs, delicate, one-of-a-kind artificial eggs, intricate in design, each of sleek gold, tapestried in colored enamel and emblazoned with jewels. Priceless, inedible, *imitation* eggs. Ma's were real.

Turning her bowl of warm, brown eggs around and around so as to get the full benefit from every side Ma said, "I really do believe that *finally* we have enough for a good big dish of creamed hard-boiled eggs for supper. We ought to have something kind of tart for dessert. Is there any of that rhubarb and strawberry preserve left? Look behind Fannie Farmer."

Over the succeeding years Nelson has changed little; it's still bony, lean and stringy. As one batch of old cross-grained types die out, they are replaced by another crop, younger, but equally cross-grained. And the new types hang on no matter how tough conditions are — another pithy core of diehards who won't be blasted loose.

Tolman Pond looks exactly the same as it did when Ma first saw it, bland and beautiful. Its wooded shoreline is the same; its basin is the same, though the contents aren't the same but a refill, all new water molded into the same old shape by the boundaries of the shore — all fresh water from the springs up the hill. Even the fish aren't the same; they're another generation, distant progeny of the ones Ma claimed by eminent domain.

The farmhouse, like the Pond, still looks the same. Ma's descendants have inherited it, inherited its sags, its leaks, its battered chimneys. The porch is still overloaded with vines; there are a couple of cracked boards that need replacing, and so on. The fields are still sour and luxuriously strewn with granite. If the farmhouse hasn't changed in appearance, neither has it in character; it is as brown and stubborn as ever. But the contents aren't the same. Like the pond, it has had a refill, all new. The original boarders have gone where all good boarders go, but the stock remains — that reliable perennial backlog of summer guests; their roots go deep.

The fences have been reinforced and hold — well, almost hold — cows, pigs and an unruly goat or two. Feet pound across the uneven barn floor. Alternately, hammering and cursing go on under the floors or up on the roof; there are strong smells, an uproar of vitality.

A large pig, tinted and fleshed out like a Rubens nude, lumbers across the lawn talking to himself and prospecting the scene with his nose. He sniffs the air from the pond, its fresh coolness, its marshy odor, then turns to sample the smells of the farmhouse. They are good, familiar. He snorkles among the fallen apples and takes an experimental nibble of Ma's asparagus plant sheltering under the old-fashioned rosebush. But nothing has quite the lure of those smells from the kitchen — beans? pies? — warm and delicious. He rumbles towards the door with a piggy ambition of hoisting his weight up for a handout. But some atavistic instinct warns him that there are boards in the porch that may not be reliable. With a resigned grunt, he joins a couple of frowsty hens napping in the shade under the porch.